SAMS
Teach You
NOTEBOOK BASICS

G000096236

Joe Kraynak

in 10 Minutes

SAMS

A Division of Macmillan Computer Publishing
201 West 103rd St., Indianapolis, Indiana, 46290 USA

Sams Teach Yourself Notebook Basics in 10 Minutes

Copyright © 1999 by Sams

All rights reserved. No part of this book shall be reproduced, stored in a retrieval system, or transmitted by any means, electronic, mechanical, photocopying, recording, or otherwise, without written permission from the publisher. No patent liability is assumed with respect to the use of the information contained herein. Although every precaution has been taken in the preparation of this book, the publisher and author assume no responsibility for errors or omissions. Neither is any liability assumed for damages resulting from the use of the information contained herein.

International Standard Book Number: 0-672-31539-4

Library of Congress Catalog Card Number: 98-89974

Printed in the United States of America

First Printing: March 1999

01   00   99   4   3   2   1

EXECUTIVE EDITOR
Angie Wethington

ACQUISITIONS EDITOR
Jamie Milazzo

DEVELOPMENT EDITOR
Nick Goetz

MANAGING EDITOR
Thomas F. Hayes

PROJECT EDITOR
Leah Kirkpatrick

COPY EDITOR
Heather Urschel

INDEXER
Greg Pearson

PROOFREADER
Mary Ellen Stephenson

TECHNICAL EDITOR
Jeff Sloan

PRODUCTION
Cheryl Lynch
Louis Porter, Jr.

Table of Contents

Dedication

To my daughter, Ali, for her inspiring joy.

Acknowledgments

Special thanks to the editors who developed, polished, and perfected this book: Jamie Milazzo, for choosing me to write this book; Nick Goetz, for making sure the book covered the most common notebook computing tasks; Jeff Sloan, for ensuring the technical accuracy of the book; Heather Kaufman Urschel, who made sure the text was concise and accurate; and Leah Kirkpatrick, for expertly shepherding this book through production. Thanks also to the production department at Macmillan Computer Publishing for transforming my stack of loose pages and pictures into an attractive, bound book.

Trademarks

All terms mentioned in this book that are known to be trademarks or service marks have been appropriately capitalized. Sams cannot attest to the accuracy of this information. Use of a term in this book should not be regarded as affecting the validity of any trademark or service mark.

Tell Us What You Think!

As the reader of this book, *you* are our most important critic and commentator. We value your opinion and want to know what we're doing right, what we could do better, what areas you'd like to see us publish in, and any other words of wisdom you're willing to pass our way.

As the Executive Editor for the General Desktop Applications team at Macmillan Computer Publishing, I welcome your comments. You can fax, email, or write me directly to let me know what you did or didn't like about this book—as well as what we can do to make our books stronger.

Please note that I cannot help you with technical problems related to the topic of this book, and that due to the high volume of mail I receive, I might not be able to reply to every message.

When you write, please be sure to include this book's title and author as well as your name and phone or fax number. I will carefully review your comments and share them with the author and editors who worked on the book.

Fax: 317-581-4770

Email: office_sams@mcp.com

Mail: Executive Editor
                General Desktop Applications
                Macmillan Computer Publishing
                201 West 103rd Street
                Indianapolis, IN 46290 USA

Introduction

Notebooks are no longer the weak species in the computer jungle. Although light and compact, notebooks nearly equal their desktop siblings in power and features and far exceed them in portability. In addition, they commonly offer plug-and-play features that make them the envy of the personal computer market.

But now that you own a notebook, you face some unique computing issues that you never had to deal with when using a desktop PC, issues that might inspire the following questions:

- How do I install and charge the battery?

- How do I connect a mouse, a full-size keyboard, or a larger monitor?

- How do I conserve battery power?

- How do I safely insert and remove PC cards?

- How do I change the dialing preferences for my modem when I'm on a trip?

- How do I transfer files between my desktop and notebook PCs?

- How do I connect to my desktop PC or network when I'm on the road?

- How do I check my email when I travel out of the state or country?

Most general computing books don't address these questions. They omit the step-by-step instructions you need to master your notebook and fully exploit its power. You need a book that shows you the basics, that teaches you specifically how to use and configure your notebook, and that won't weigh you down when you're on the road.

Welcome to *Sams Teach Yourself Notebook Basics in 10 Minutes*

Sams Teach Yourself Notebook Basics in 10 Minutes is your notebook companion, providing all the answers and instructions you need to confidently perform essential notebook computing tasks. This slim volume doesn't bog you down with excessive jabber about general computing. Instead, it covers the most essential notebook tasks:

- Setting up your notebook and installing add-on equipment.
- Using the compact keyboard and configuring the unique pointing devices.
- Conserving battery power.
- Safely installing and removing PC cards.
- Communicating with infrared (wireless) devices.
- Using a docking station to make your notebook act like a desktop PC.
- Transferring files between your notebook and desktop PC using a floppy disk or a direct cable connection.
- Connecting to your desktop PC or network via modem.
- Checking your email and connecting to the Internet when you're on the road.
- Maintaining and enhancing your notebook.
- Securing your notebook to prevent theft.

And that's not all. I've also thrown in coverage of some slightly more advanced topics. Near the end of this book, you'll find instructions for using your notebook to give business presentations when you're on the road, configuring your notebook by changing its BIOS settings, and using your notebook in your car to obtain directions via satellite!

To make this book even more valuable as a travel companion, I've included three appendixes that reveal the ever-growing market of notebook toys and accessories, provide contact information for notebook suppliers, and give you the tech support numbers of the most popular notebook manufacturers. With this information, you'll no longer have to call home when you run into trouble on the road.

Who Should Use *Sams Teach Yourself Notebook Basics in 10 Minutes?*

People who own notebooks are typically busier than desktop PC owners. You have bags to pack, clients to visit, and planes to catch. You don't have the luxury of sitting down uninterrupted for hours at a time to learn everything about your notebook.

Sams Teach Yourself Notebook Basics in 10 Minutes doesn't attempt to teach you everything about your notebook, its operating system, your modem, or email and Internet connections. Instead, it focuses on the tasks that are unique to notebooks and covers these tasks in bite-sized chunks, giving you quick access to the information you need right now.

How to Use This Book

Sams Teach Yourself Notebook Basics in 10 Minutes covers each task in a single, self-contained lesson that's designed to take 10 minutes or less to complete. Without relying on technical jargon, this book provides straightforward, easy-to-follow explanations, lots of pictures, and numbered lists that show you which keys to press and which options to select.

Of course, you can read this book from cover to cover and perform each task in sequence. However, when you're in a hurry, don't feel obligated to read everything. Use the *To Do list* on the inside front cover or the Table of Contents at the beginning of the book to find the task you need, and then follow the step-by-step instructions to complete the task. To track down more specific information, check out the comprehensive index at the back of this book.

Icons and Conventions

This book includes an abundant supply of the following icons to point out useful tips, cautions, notes, and other important tidbits:

 Tips highlight shortcuts and hints for performing a task more quickly and efficiently.

 Cautions alert you to possible problems and show you how to avoid the most common pitfalls.

 Plain English elements define technical terms and other jargon that commonly trip up new users.

LESSON 1

Setting Up Your Notebook (The Basics)

This lesson shows you how to install a battery and connect the power cable and basic external devices to your notebook.

Because a notebook combines the monitor, system unit, keyboard, pointing device, and speakers into a single case, setting up a notebook is fairly easy. However, unpacking and setting up your notebook introduces some unique issues and safety concerns. This lesson shows you how to set up your notebook safely and properly.

Unpacking Your Notebook

When you get your notebook home, unpack it carefully. Avoid cutting into the box because you might inadvertently hack through a cable or scratch the case. Check the box thoroughly to make sure that you received everything recorded on the packing list. You need the following essential equipment to get started:

- The notebook itself.

- A battery specifically designed for your notebook.

- The AC adapter (power cord) specifically designed for your notebook. (Using the wrong adapter can damage your notebook.)

- External disk drives (if included). Many notebooks include a drive bay that allows you to connect either a floppy or CD-ROM drive, but both cannot be connected at the same time.

After unpacking your notebook, let it become acclimated to the environment for three to four hours. Sudden changes in temperature and humidity can cause moisture to form inside the unit, which could damage your notebook when you turn on the power. While you're waiting, take a tour of your notebook, connect any additional devices that came with it, and read through its documentation.

 Keep the Box   Keep the box and packing material that came with your notebook for at least the warranty period. Many manufacturers do not allow you to return your notebook without the original box. In addition, the box and packing material offer the best protection for your notebook when you ship it or move it.

Getting to Know Your Notebook

Most notebooks are designed like briefcases with a hinge on the back. To open the notebook, slide the latch(es) on the front or press the release button and lift the cover. This gives you access to the monitor, the built-in pointing device, and the keyboard.

Notebooks pack all components into a single case, which can make components and ports difficult to locate. To further complicate matters, manufacturers position the components to save space, decrease weight, and conserve power rather than to make them convenient. Use the following list and Figure 1.1 to track down the basic components of *your* notebook:

- The monitor is the top half of your notebook.

- The keyboard takes up most of the bottom half of the notebook.

- The power button can be located on or near the display, above the keyboard, or on the side of the case. On some notebooks, you must slide open a panel for access to the button. See Lesson 3, "Turning Your Notebook On and Off," for details.

- The built-in pointing device can be a touchpad, trackball, TrackPoint (a little lever smack dab in the middle of the keyboard), or built-in mouse.

- The battery compartment is typically located on the underside or side of the notebook.

- Speakers can be located near the monitor or just above the keyboard.

- The microphone is normally marked by a tiny hole in the top or bottom half of the notebook. Look for a small microphone icon.

- The drive bay is typically located on the keyboard half of the notebook. (Newer notebooks might omit the drive bay to save space and reduce weight. You connect the drive using a cable.)

- PC card slots are typically located on the left or right side of the keyboard half of the notebook. Lesson 8, "Inserting and Removing PC (PCMCIA) Cards," shows you how to install and remove PC cards.

PCMCIA Short for Personal Computer Memory Card International Association, a PCMCIA card is a credit-card sized circuit board that you insert in to a special slot on your notebook to add more memory, a modem, a network adapter, or other devices. This book refers to these cards simply as *PC cards*.

- The LCD indicator panel is typically located just above the keyboard and displays icons that convey information about the notebook's operation, including whether the unit is plugged in or is operating on batteries, when NumLock or CapsLock is on, when a PC card or drive is working, or when the machine is in sleep mode.

No Two Notebooks Are Created Equal Notebook components vary greatly. Your notebook might not have all the components listed here or might have additional components.

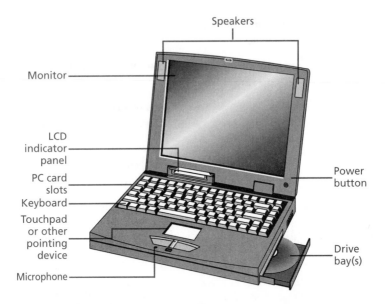

FIGURE 1.1   Find the corresponding components on your note-book.

Locating the All-Important Ports

Although the most essential PC components are built right into the note-book case, the notebook cannot possibly house all components. To give the notebook further expandability, notebooks commonly include *ports*.

 Port   An outlet into which you can plug an external device, such as a printer, mouse, monitor, or modem.

Ports are typically located on the back of the keyboard half of the note-book and/or on the left side. You might need to flip open a panel to locate them. The following list and Figure 1.2 describe the ports most commonly built into a notebook:

• A parallel port is commonly used to connect a printer or external drive, such as a floppy or zip drive.

- A serial port is typically used to connect an optional mouse or external modem.

- A standard VGA port enables you to connect to an external monitor or projector.

- PS/2 ports enable you to connect an external (full-size) keyboard and/or a mouse. (Look on the back and sides of the notebook for the PS/2 port[s]).

- One or more USB ports are included on most newer notebooks, and enable you to connect several USB devices to a single port. USB devices include printers, mice, keyboards, and scanners.

 USB Short for *Universal Serial Bus*, USB is a relatively new standard that enables you to connect devices in a *daisy-chain configuration* and safely connect and disconnect devices when the notebook is on. With USB, you can connect up to 127 devices to a single port!

 Daisy-Chain Configuration A daisy-chain configuration consists of several devices typically connected one to the next in a series. For example, you can plug a USB keyboard into the USB port, plug a USB printer into the keyboard, and then plug a USB external drive into the printer.

- An infrared (IrDA) port is typically covered by a rectangular piece of translucent plastic. This port provides wireless communications between the notebook and infrared devices, such as network cards, printers, and keyboards.

- Multimedia jacks, commonly located on the left side of the keyboard half, enable you to connect a standard microphone or speakers to upgrade the sound system. (Older notebooks might not include these jacks.)

- Video In and/or Video Out ports (available on a few notebooks) enable the notebook to display data on a TV or receive data from a TV or camcorder.

- An expansion port is a wider port typically used to connect the notebook to a docking station or port replicator so that you can use the notebook as you would use a desktop PC. See Lesson 10, "Plugging into a Docking Station or Port Replicator."

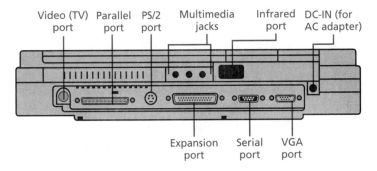

FIGURE 1.2   Ports enable you to connect additional devices to your notebook.

 Crank Up the Volume   Your notebook should have a volume control near the multimedia jacks.

Because modem standards change so frequently, few notebooks come with a built-in modem. If your notebook has a phone jack, it might or might not have a built-in modem. In some cases, the manufacturer offers an optional modem; if you choose not to purchase the modem, the manufacturer might install a modemless jack only to block the hole in the case. If you try to use the jack, you won't get a dial tone. If there is no phone jack, you can add a modem by installing a PC card modem or connecting an external modem to the serial port.

Choosing an Appropriate Location to Work

When you're traveling, you might have few choices on where to set up camp with your notebook. When possible, choose a comfortable location that is safe for your notebook. The following guidelines can help you pick an appropriate work area:

- Place the notebook on a sturdy surface at a level convenient for typing. Your wrists should not have to reach up to type, nor should you have to look down at the screen. This is tough with a notebook.

- Make sure air can freely circulate around your notebook. Excessive heat can damage the sensitive components inside the case. Do not place your notebook in direct sunlight.

- Keep your notebook away from any electromagnetic or radio frequency interference emitted by devices such as televisions, stereo speakers, copying machines, phones, and air conditioners.

- When using the AC adapter, make sure the power cord is out of the way so that nobody will trip over it.

- Clean and dust the work area to prevent dust from building up in ports and inside the notebook.

- Make sure your work area is near a power outlet that is not on the same circuit as a major appliance, such as an air conditioner, washing machine, or refrigerator. Power fluctuations can cause data loss and damage components.

- If you're using a modem, house your notebook near a phone jack.

Installing the Battery

Most notebooks come with at least one battery. Although the manufacturer might have charged the battery before shipping the notebook, you should install the battery and charge it to ensure that it is fully charged when you need it. The charger is typically built into the notebook. To install the battery, take the following steps:

1. If you already plugged in and turned on your notebook, turn it off.

 Turn It Off!   Before removing or installing a battery, make sure the notebook is turned off. Some notebooks enable you to swap batteries when the power is on, but check your documentation—don't take chances.

2. Close the lid.

3. If the battery compartment is at the bottom of the notebook, carefully turn the notebook over and set it on a flat surface. Some notebooks feature convenient access to the battery pack at the front or side of the case.

4. If the battery compartment has a cover, remove the cover. Although some battery covers might be secured with a screw, most have a sliding latch to release the cover.

 Be Gentle   When turning over your notebook, be careful not to bump any connectors or open panels. Some plastic access panels crack easily.

5. Position the battery so that the contacts on the battery match up with the contacts in the battery compartment (see Figure 1.3).

6. Gently slide the battery in place and follow the manufacturer's instructions on how to secure the battery in its compartment.

7. If you removed a cover from the battery compartment in step 4, replace the cover now and secure it in place.

8. If you turned the notebook over in step 3, gently turn it right-side-up to rest on its base.

Figure 1.3   Load the battery into the battery compartment.

After installing the battery, take a look at the LCD display on your notebook. It should display a battery icon that indicates the level of charge. When you connect the AC adapter to the notebook and a power source later in this lesson, the LCD battery icon should indicate that the battery is charging. If the LCD does not indicate that a battery is loaded, repeat the steps to reload the battery.

 Use the Right Batteries   Use only batteries that are specifically designed for your notebook. Using the wrong battery can damage your notebook and void its warranty.

Connecting Your Disk Drives

To save space and reduce the weight of notebooks, designers have concocted a wide variety of configurations for connecting disk drives to notebooks. Use the following list to determine the configuration you have and refer to your notebook's documentation for specific instructions on how to install additional drives:

- The hard drive is typically built into the keyboard half of the notebook. Most newer notebooks contain a swappable hard drive that you can insert and remove like a battery.

- Most notebooks come with a built-in CD-ROM or DVD drive or provide a drive bay into which you can insert a CD-ROM or floppy disk drive. Some notebooks even enable you to install a second battery in the swappable bay.

- Compact notebooks can include external CD-ROM or floppy disk drives that you connect to the notebook with a cable. You can connect the drive to a special drive port or to the parallel port. Check your notebook's documentation for instructions specific to your notebook.

- Many notebooks include a built-in CD-ROM or floppy disk drive and enable you to connect an additional drive to the parallel port.

- You can install additional external drives by installing a special PC card that acts as a drive controller card. You can purchase PC cards that function as small hard drives, complete with a disk.

Figure 1.4 shows a typical notebook set up with an internal CD-ROM drive and an external floppy disk drive connected to the parallel printer port.

 Power Off!   Before connecting a disk drive to your notebook, make sure the power is off.

Hard drive is
enclosed in the case

CD-ROM
drive

Optional floppy disk
drive connected to
parallel port

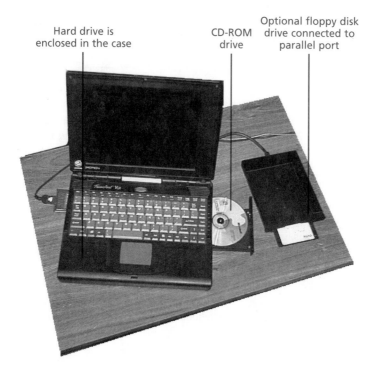

FIGURE 1.4   Most notebooks have a built-in hard drive, a CD-ROM
drive, and an optional floppy disk drive.

Plugging in the AC Adapter

Before you can start using your notebook, you must connect it to the AC
adapter and plug the adapter into a power outlet. Take the following steps:

1. Plug a surge suppressor power strip or adapter into a three-
   pronged, grounded power outlet.

2. Plug the AC adapter that came with your notebook into the surge
   suppressor.

3. Plug the AC adapter into the notebook's DC IN power outlet, which is typically located on the back of the notebook.

 Use the Right AC Adapter   Use only the AC adapter that came with your notebook or an adapter specifically approved by the manufacturer. Because AC adapters have different voltage ratings, using the wrong adapter can cook your system, destroy the battery, or ruin the adapter.

In this lesson, you learned how to unpack your notebook and connect basic devices, including the battery and disk drives. The next lesson shows you how to connect a printer, external keyboard, mouse, monitor, speakers, and other optional devices.

LESSON 2
Connecting Additional Equipment and Devices

This lesson teaches you how to connect a printer, external keyboard, mouse, monitor, speakers, and other optional devices to your notebook.

The back and sides of your notebook are populated with ports and jacks that enable you to connect your notebook to other external devices, called peripherals. These ports expand the capabilities of your notebook, enabling it to act more like a desktop PC. In this lesson, you learn how to connect a printer, keyboard, mouse, monitor, speakers, and additional peripherals.

Turn Off the Power Before Connecting Unless your notebook's documentation specifies otherwise, always turn off the notebook before connecting or disconnecting any cables. Some ports and PC card slots support hot swapping, but check the documentation to be sure.

Hot Swapping Hot swapping consists of connecting devices to a PC while it is on. USB ports and most PCMCIA (PC card) slots support hot swapping, which means you can disconnect one device and connect another without turning the power on or off.

Connecting a Printer to Your Notebook

Notebooks provide several options for connecting a printer:

- The parallel port enables you to connect the notebook to the printer using a standard parallel printer cable.

- An infrared port supports wireless communications to a printer that has a compatible infrared port. See Lesson 9, "Communicating with Infrared (Wireless) Devices."

- The USB port provides a connection to a USB-capable printer, as explained later in this lesson.

To connect your notebook to a printer using a standard parallel printer cable, take the following steps:

1. Make sure the power to the notebook and printer is off.

2. Plug the 25-pin, D-shaped connector into the notebook's parallel port, as shown in Figure 2.1.

3. Plug the Centronics 36 (flat) connector into the matching port on the printer and snap the bail wires in place (if present) to secure the connection.

 Centronics Connector   A Centronics connector is a long, narrow plug that has a row of contacts instead of pins. This is the standard connector used for parallel printers and other parallel devices.

4. Make sure the printer has paper and turn on the printer.

5. Turn on your notebook.

6. In Windows, click the Start button, point to Settings, and click Printers.

7. Click or double-click the Add New Printer icon and follow the onscreen instructions to install the software for the printer.

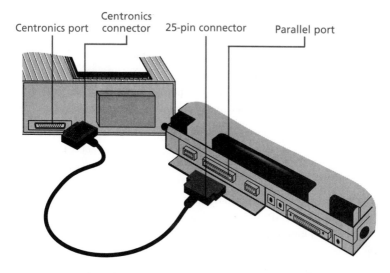

Centronics port   Centronics connector   25-pin connector   Parallel port

FIGURE 2.1 Plug the 25-pin connector on the printer cable into the parallel printer port.

 Share a Printer If you have a desktop PC that's already connected to the printer you want to use, you might be able to set up a direct cable connection between your notebook and desktop PC and share the printer. See Lesson 13, "Connecting Your Notebook and Desktop PCs," for details.

Plugging in a Full-Size Keyboard

When you're putting in a couple of hours of work on the road, the dinky notebook keyboard is sufficient. However, if you plan on doing a full day's work, you'll want some room to spread out. Fortunately, most notebooks can accommodate a full-size keyboard via the USB or PS/2 keyboard port.

In most cases, the connection is obvious, as shown in Figure 2.2, but your notebook might have a more complicated configuration:

- If your notebook has only one PS/2 port, it can accommodate a keyboard, mouse, or both. Using a Y-connector, you can connect both your keyboard and mouse to a single port.

- If your notebook has two PS/2 ports, make sure you plug the keyboard into the keyboard port, not the mouse port. On some notebooks, it doesn't matter, but on others the keyboard cannot function when it is plugged into the mouse port.

- If you have a USB keyboard, plug it into the notebook's USB port. If you have more than one USB device, but your notebook has only one USB port, you can connect a multi-port USB hub to the notebook and then connect two or more devices to the hub. Some USB devices, such as printers and monitors, have built-in hubs for connecting additional devices.

Connect a Keyboard and Mouse   If your notebook has only one PS/2 port, purchase a special keyboard that has a mouse attached to it or a built-in trackball. Another option is to connect a serial mouse to the serial port, instead of the PS/2 port, or purchase an adapter that enables you to plug your PS/2 mouse into the serial port.

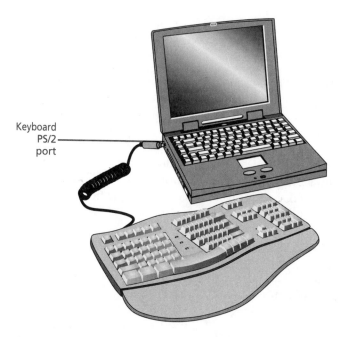

FIGURE 2.2   Most notebooks have a PS/2 port into which you can plug a full-size keyboard.

Plugging in a Mouse

Notebook designers haven't yet developed the perfect pointing device; a mouse is far superior to a touchpad, TrackPoint, or trackball. Fortunately, most notebooks feature a serial or PS/2 port for connecting a standard mouse. Most notebooks offer one or more of the following options:

- A PS/2 port for connecting a standard keyboard, a PS/2 style mouse, or trackball.

- A 9-pin serial port for plugging in a serial mouse. (If you have a PS/2 style mouse, you can purchase an adapter that lets you plug it into a 9-pin serial port.)

- A USB mouse that connects to the USB port on the notebook or a USB port on a device that's connected to the notebook.

To connect the mouse, simply plug it into the matching port. When you turn on your notebook, Windows typically recognizes that a mouse is connected to the notebook and leads you through the process of installing the required software. If Windows does not initiate the installation and the mouse doesn't work, run the Add New Hardware Wizard from the Windows Control Panel.

 Disable the Touchpad In most cases, you can use both the mouse and the built-in pointing device. However, if the devices conflict or you want to disable one of the devices, refer to Lesson 5, "Dealing with Touchpads and Other Pointing Devices," for details.

Connecting a Standard Monitor

Like the diminutive notebook keyboard, the screen is sufficient for travel but substandard for daily use. If you are using your notebook as a desktop PC, consider purchasing a 17-inch or larger monitor and connecting it to your notebook, as shown in Figure 2.3. Remember to turn off the notebook and monitor before making the connection. See Lesson 6, "Changing Your Notebook's Display Settings," for specific instructions for installing an external monitor.

 DO NOT Place the Monitor on Your Notebook You might be tempted to place the monitor on the closed notebook case, as you can on a desktop PC. Don't do it: You could crack the case.

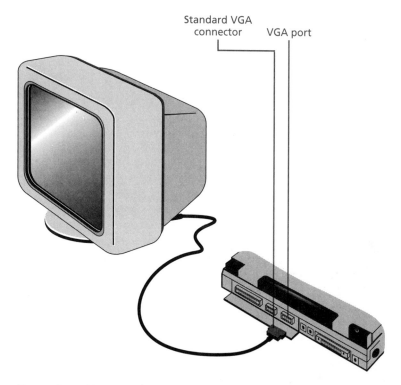

FIGURE 2.3   You can plug a standard monitor into the VGA port.

Improving Your Notebook's Audio System

Compared to the high-quality audio output of current desktop systems, notebook audio sounds like a scratchy phonograph. Fortunately, most notebooks feature a microphone input jack and audio output jacks that enable you to connect a high-quality microphone and amplified stereo speakers. Take the following steps and refer to Figure 2.4 to make the proper connections:

1. If desired, plug a standard microphone into the MIC IN jack.

2. Plug a set of headphones or amplified speakers into the AUDIO OUT jack.

3. To record audio clips, plug in an audio player such as a CD player into the AUDIO IN jack.

4. Turn on your notebook, insert your favorite audio CD, and adjust the volume as desired.

 Adjust the Volume You can adjust the volume using any of several controls. Use the dial on your notebook, the controls on the amplified speakers, and the Windows volume control. To access the volume controls in Windows, click the speaker icon on the far right of the taskbar.

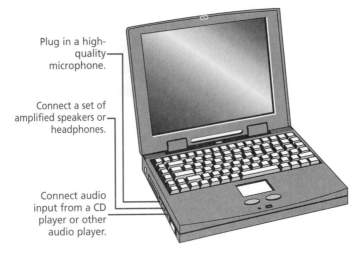

Plug in a high-quality microphone.

Connect a set of amplified speakers or headphones.

Connect audio input from a CD player or other audio player.

FIGURE 2.4 Don't expect theater-quality sound, but you can improve your notebook's audio output considerably.

Using the Video Out Port

Few notebooks feature external video output. However, if your notebook has a round jack, called an RCA, S-video, or composite video jack, you might be able to output video to a standard VCR or TV. This is especially useful for business presentations. Check your notebook's documentation to determine the type of cable(s) you need.

To make the necessary connections, take the following steps:

1. Make sure the notebook and video device are off.

2. Plug the connector on one end of the video cable into the desired jack on the video device.

3. Plug the connector on the other end of the cable into the VIDEO OUT jack on your notebook, as shown in Figure 2.5.

4. Turn on the video device and then turn on your notebook.

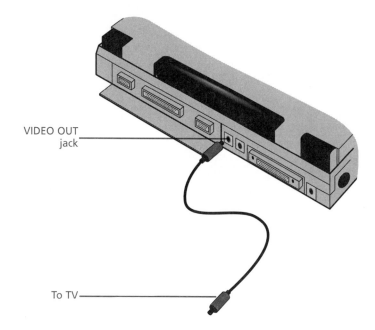

FIGURE 2.5   Plug the video cable into the VIDEO OUT jack on your notebook.

 Use a Short Cable   For best video quality, use a video cable no longer than 20 feet.

Video Quality Varies   When outputting video to a TV, the video quality varies depending on the TV. You might need to adjust the settings on the TV and your notebook for optimum display.

If you're planning on watching TV on your notebook, don't get your hopes up—most notebooks are not cable-ready. However, you can purchase a PC card to add video input capabilities to your notebook.

Connecting USB Devices

The ultimate in plug-and-play technology, USB enables you to install devices without turning off your computer or using a screwdriver. You plug the component in to the USB port and it works. USB enables you to connect up to 127 devices to a single port. You can daisy-chain the devices with cables up to five meters long or connect a USB *hub*, which contains several USB ports. Figure 2.6 shows a USB monitor that has a built-in USB port at its base.

You can connect nearly any type of device that supports USB into a USB port, including a keyboard, mouse, printer, scanner, monitor, or disk drive. In addition, most USB devices do not require a separate power cable because the USB cable carries the power. This cuts down on the number of cables you need to connect (and untangle).

To connect a USB device to your notebook, take the following steps:

1. If the device has a power cable, plug the cable into your surge suppressor power strip.

2. Align the flat end of the USB cable with your notebook's USB port and gently insert the connector.

3. Match the connector on opposite end of the cable with the shape of the USB port on the device and gently insert the connector. If this is the first time you connected the device, Windows prompts you to install the software for the device.

4. Follow the onscreen instructions to install the required software from the Windows CD or from the disk that came with the device.

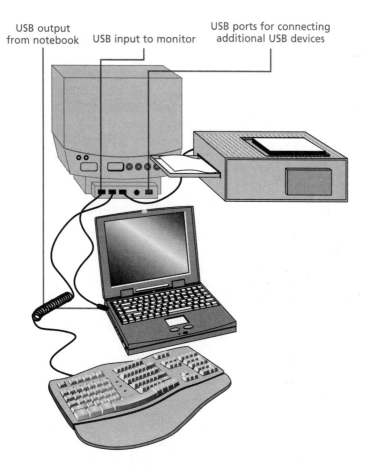

USB output from notebook   USB input to monitor   USB ports for connecting additional USB devices

FIGURE 2.6   USB devices commonly have their own USB hubs.

You must install the software (driver) for the device only once. You can then disconnect and connect the device as desired, even with the power on, and Windows will identify the device and be prepared to use it.

 Add USB Ports to Your Notebook   If your notebook does not have a USB port, you can install a PC card that adds one or two USB ports. Check out ADS Technologies at www.adstech.com for details and information about additional USB products, including USB hubs.

In this lesson, you learned how to connect a printer, external keyboard, mouse, monitor, and speakers to your notebook. The next lesson shows you how to properly turn your notebook on and off.

LESSON 3

Turning Your Notebook On and Off

This lesson shows you how to turn your notebook on and off safely, rouse it from sleep mode, and properly care for the battery.

Turning your notebook on and off might seem like a no-brainer: You press and release the power button. However, if you fail to follow the steps in the proper sequence, your notebook might not identify peripheral devices on startup and can lose data or damage the hard drive on shutdown. This lesson shows you how to start and shut down your notebook properly and provides important information on caring for your battery.

Turning On Your Notebook

The only difficult step in turning on your notebook is finding the power button. On most notebooks, the button is just above the keyboard. On others, the button might be on the side or back and might be hidden behind a sliding cover to prevent you from accidentally pressing it. To turn on your notebook, follow these steps:

1. Turn on any devices that are connected to your notebook. (If the devices are not on, your notebook might fail to identify them.)

2. If a floppy disk drive is connected to your notebook, make sure it is empty. (If the drive contains a disk, your notebook might try to boot from that disk.)

 Boot When your notebook boots, it reads its startup instructions, performs a series of internal checks, and loads the operating system. The operating system, such as Windows, is the basic software your notebook uses to run other programs.

3. Press and hold down the power button for one or two seconds until the power light comes on or the LCD panel displays an icon indicating that the power is on (see Figure 3.1).

LCD display ———   Power
                                                                  button

FIGURE 3.1   Press and hold down the power button for one or two seconds.

As your notebook jumps into action, it displays a series of messages as it performs its internal diagnostics. If your notebook uses Windows as its operating system, the Windows logo appears and then the Windows desktop appears, as shown in Figure 3.2.

Be Patient   Your notebook might take a minute or so to start up and display the opening screen. Never turn off the power until the opening screen appears.

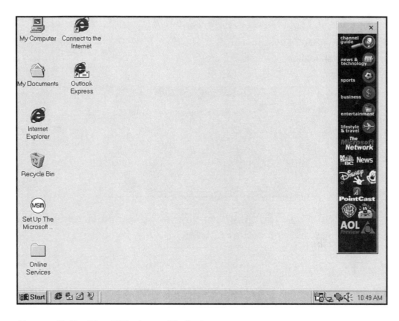

FIGURE 3.2   The Windows 98 desktop.

Turning Off Your Notebook

It's tempting to just press the power button when you're done working. Resist the urge. Powering down improperly can cause data loss, damage important system files, or even harm your hard disk drive. Take these steps to shut down properly:

1. In any applications you are using, choose File, Save to save your work.

2. Exit any applications that are currently running.

3. Click the Start button in the lower-left corner of the Windows desktop and click Shut Down. The Shut Down Windows dialog box appears, as shown in Figure 3.3.

FIGURE 3.3 When you choose to shut down, Windows provides several shutdown and restart options.

4. Click one of the following options:

> Shut Down shuts down Windows so that you can safely turn off your notebook or turns off the power automatically.
>
> Stand By (Windows 98) places your notebook in power-saving mode without completely shutting it down. When you want to use your notebook again, press the Shift key or the power button on your notebook.
>
> Suspend (Windows 95 or NT) is Stand By mode for Windows 95 and NT. It places your notebook in power-saving mode. When you want to use your notebook again, press the Shift key or the power button on your notebook.

5. Click OK. Windows automatically turns off your notebook or displays a message indicating that it is now safe to turn off your computer. If you chose Stand By, the screen goes blank, but the power remains on.

6. Check the LCD panel or the hard drive indicator light to make sure your hard drive is not active. (Turning off the power when the disk is spinning can damage it.)

7. If you chose to shut down completely, wait until the message appears indicating that it is safe to turn off your computer and then press and hold down the power button for one or two seconds to turn it off. (Don't perform this step if you chose Stand By.)

Don't Waste Power   If you have USB devices connected to your notebook, they might continue to use power from your notebook even when it is off. Disconnect the devices to conserve energy and battery power.

Don't Close Your Notebook When It's On   Many notebooks automatically shut down when you snap the lid shut, causing an improper shut down. In most cases, the notebook sounds a loud beep before shutting down. Reopen the notebook and shut down properly.

Waking Your Notebook from Sleep Mode

Most notebooks have a built-in power-saving feature that automatically shuts down the hard drive, display, and other power-hungry components after a certain period of inactivity. The LCD should display an icon that indicates the notebook is in sleep mode. To rouse the notebook, press the Shift key, tap the touchpad, or roll the mouse and wait 20–30 seconds.

If pressing a key or activating the pointer does not wake your notebook, you might have one of the few notebooks that requires you to press the power button. Be careful: On most notebooks, pressing the power button when the notebook is in sleep mode turns off the notebook. Check your documentation before using the power button to wake your notebook.

System Lockup? If your notebook doesn't wake up, it might be locked up. Restart your notebook as explained in the next section and then check the power-saving settings, as explained in Lesson 7, "Conserving Battery Power." In some cases, the notebook's power-saving features conflict with the Windows power-saving features, causing the notebook to lock up. For a permanent fix, you might need to disable one or more power-saving features in your system settings, as explained in Lesson 22, "Checking Your Notebook's BIOS Settings."

Safely Restarting Your Notebook

Every PC, including your notebook, is susceptible to system lockups. The mouse pointer doesn't move, you can't type, or the screen goes completely blank. If you turn off the power, you risk losing data and damaging system files. To safely restart, try the following techniques:

- Wait a couple of minutes for the application to complete whatever task it might be in the process of performing.

- If Windows is still locked up, press Ctrl+Alt+Delete. A list of currently running applications appears, as shown in Figure 3.4. Click the application that has (not responding) next to its name and then click the End Task button. If prompted to confirm, click End Task. This usually closes the problem application and returns control to Windows.

- If pressing Ctrl+Alt+Delete does not work, try to save any work you've done in your other applications, exit from them (to prevent losing documents or changes), and then press Ctrl+Alt+Delete again and try to close the problem application.

- If your system is still locked up, press Ctrl+Alt+Delete and then click the Shut Down button or press Ctrl+Alt+Delete again. This restarts Windows.

- If the condition persists, press your notebook's reset button. If your notebook has no reset button, turn off your notebook, wait at least one minute, and turn it back on.

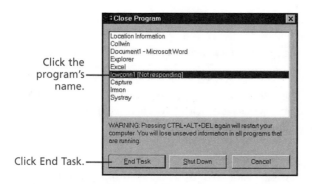

Click the program's name.

Click End Task.

FIGURE 3.4 Windows might let you close a program without shutting down Windows.

If you shut down Windows or restart your notebook to correct the problem, Windows might automatically run ScanDisk on startup to repair any files or folders that might have been damaged by an improper shutdown.

Taking Care of Your Battery

When you first start using your notebook, you might have several questions regarding the battery: Should I keep the battery in the notebook all the time? Should I let it run down completely before recharging it? How do I refresh or recondition the battery? To properly care for your battery, follow these simple guidelines:

- On first use, fully charge the battery. This can take two to three hours if the notebook is off or several hours if your notebook is on. The LCD should display an icon showing the battery's charge. Windows also displays this information, as discussed in Lesson 7, "Conserving Battery Power."

- If you keep the battery in your notebook, keep it as fully charged as possible. Don't unplug your notebook, let the battery power run down 50 percent, and then recharge the battery. Batteries live through a fixed number of charges.

- If your notebook uses a nickel cadmium battery and you partially discharge the battery, try to let it discharge completely before recharging it. If your notebook uses a nickel metal-hydride and lithium-ion battery, this is not a major concern. See the following section, "Comparing Battery Types," for details.

- Every month or so, let the battery completely run down. Unplug the AC adapter and let the battery power the system. To speed up the discharge, insert an audio CD. Save any documents and close all applications, just to be safe.

 Is It Warm?   When a battery is recharging, it is normal for the battery to feel warm.

- If your notebook runs on a lithium-ion battery, you might need to occasionally *recondition* the battery. Refer to the notebook's documentation or contact the manufacturer to determine the proper procedure for reconditioning the battery.

 Charge at Room Temperature   If a battery is too hot or too cold, it might not hold a full charge.

Comparing Battery Types

Battery performance and the steps you must take to care for your battery vary depending on the type of battery your notebook uses. The following list describes the three most common types of batteries used in notebooks (listed from most to least common):

- *LiIon (lithium-ion)* batteries are the lightest of the bunch and offer the longest battery life between charges. In addition, Lithium-ion batteries are *smart batteries*; they have a built-in memory that records what a full and empty charge "feels" like. Occasionally, you must recondition the battery to refresh its memory so that the battery can take on a full charge. This process usually takes from 12 to 24 hours.

Smart Battery   Newer batteries, called smart batteries, provide information to the notebook to help it use power more efficiently and make more precise judgments concerning how much battery power remains.

- *NiMH (nickel metal-hydride)* batteries are a step down from LiIon batteries, but have a higher storage density than NiCad batteries (covered next). The higher storage density gives NiMH batteries approximately 30 percent more power per pound than NiCad batteries.

- *NiCad (nickel cadmium)* batteries are pretty much obsolete. Not only are they heavy, but their recharge system is quirky. For example, if you frequently recharge the battery when it still has 30 percent of its power, the battery begins to "think" that at 30 percent it is completely drained. Eventually, a complete recharge gives you only 70 percent power. To refresh the battery, completely discharge it before recharging.

 Building a Better Battery   Battery manufacturers are constantly trying to build better batteries. Newer, li-polymer batteries promise to last five times longer on a single charge. Unfortunately, these batteries have a shorter life expectancy than LiIon batteries.

Your notebook might have additional built-in batteries that you rarely need to service. Some notebooks have a backup battery that acts like a reserve gas tank, giving you time to properly shut down your notebook when the main battery expires. Another battery supplies power for storing essential system settings. If you don't use your notebook for over a month, plug in the AC adapter for several hours to fully charge these batteries.

Common Battery Questions and Answers

Although it seems as though batteries should function worry free, they commonly inspire concern and questions in new users. To allay your fears and answer your questions, read through the following list of questions and answers:

- *How do I get my* new *battery to work?* New batteries are commonly shipped in a fully discharged state. Fully charge the battery for 12 to 24 hours before first using it. The first two or three times you run your notebook on battery power, fully discharge the battery before recharging it.

- *My notebook came with a nickel cadmium battery. Can I use a nickel metal-hydride battery instead?* No. Some notebook battery chargers designed for NiMH batteries can handle NiCad batteries, but NiCad chargers cannot charge NiMH batteries. Use only a battery specifically designed for your notebook. Using the wrong battery can damage the battery or the notebook or cause the battery to emit noxious fumes or explode.

- *How long will my notebook run using a fully charged battery?* You can expect your notebook to run for two to three hours on a full charge. However, the time varies greatly depending on the activity. If you're running a CD-ROM, hard drive, and other peripherals, the battery will drain much more quickly. See Lesson 7.

- *What's the average life of a battery?* You can expect your battery to last for 500–800 charges, or about one to three years. Lithium-ion batteries can last for over 1,000 charges.

- *How do I know if my battery is nearing the end of its life?* If your battery is fully charged and powers your notebook for only 20 minutes or so, that's a good sign that you need a new battery. Before retiring the battery, try completely discharging and then recharging it.

- *Can I use a separate battery charger?* Yes, but make sure the charger is designed for the type of batteries your notebook uses. Using the wrong charger can damage the battery or cause it to emit noxious fumes or explode.

Basic Battery Safety

To prevent damaging the battery or harming yourself, follow these safety precautions:

- Don't short-circuit the battery by allowing any electrical conductor (such as a paper clip) to touch two or more of the contacts at the same time.

- Don't expose the battery to moisture, which could short-circuit it.

- Don't drop the battery. The battery contains corrosive material that can leak out onto your notebook or your work area, damaging the notebook or causing severe burns.

- Keep the battery away from sources of extreme heat, which could cause the battery to explode.

- Properly dispose of the battery. Check your local computer or electronics store to see whether they accept worn out batteries. Many retailers who deal in computer batteries recycle the batteries.

In this lesson, you learned how to turn your notebook on and off, wake it from sleep mode, and restart it. You also learned how to care for your battery properly. The next lesson orients you to the notebook's compact keyboard.

LESSON 4

Navigating the Streamlined Keyboard

This lesson shows you how to use the notebook's compact keyboard and special keys.

To conserve space, notebooks use a compact keyboard on which the keys are placed closely together. Many keys serve double-duty, performing the same jobs as their standard keyboard siblings while at the same time providing access to special features. Some character keys, for example, might function as a numeric keypad, and others might be used to adjust the display's brightness and contrast. This lesson teaches you how to expertly navigate this multi-function keyboard.

Using the Standard Alphanumeric Keys

Although positioned more closely together on a notebook keyboard, the alphanumeric keys on your notebook hold the same relative positions as they do on a standard keyboard. However, because your fingers don't change their spacing, reorienting yourself to the keyboard can be quite a chore. Figure 4.1 highlights the alphanumeric keys.

FIGURE 4.1 The relative positions of the alphanumeric keys are the same as on a standard keyboard.

Ergonomic Concerns Unless you have a fancy IBM butterfly keyboard, which spreads out to give you more space, your notebook keyboard forces your wrists to bend unnaturally as you reach in to type. This can result in a killer case of carpal tunnel syndrome. If you plan on typing for extended periods, connect a full-size keyboard, as explained in Lesson 2, "Connecting Additional Equipment and Devices." An ergonomic or split keyboard is the best choice.

Accessing Special Functions with the Fn Key

The Fn (Function) key enables you to use other keys on the keyboard to perform special tasks. Think of it as an Alt key for configuring your system. The Fn key is typically located in the lower-left corner of the keyboard and is marked with a different color than is used for most of the other keys, for example, the Fn might be blue instead of white or black. Keys that perform a special function when used with the Fn key have their special function printed in a color matching that of the Fn key (see Figure 4.2).

Primary function is
printed in white or black.

Special function is printed in
a color that matches the Fn key.

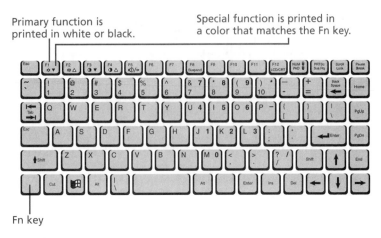

Fn key

FIGURE 4.2 The Fn key enables other keys to serve a dual
purpose.

To use keys to perform their special functions, such as increasing or
decreasing the display contrast, hold down the Fn key while pressing the
special function key.

 Write Down the Less Obvious Keystrokes Before
you take your notebook on the road, write down the
Fn keystrokes that are less obvious and tuck them
away in your carrying case. If you forget your notebook's documentation, you can quickly refer to your
list for help.

 Troubleshooting Pressing some Fn+key combinations can cause your screen to go blank or disable the
internal speakers. These key combinations tell your
notebook to send output to external devices rather
than to internal devices. If you press one of these key
combinations by mistake, simply press the keys again.

Activating the Numeric Keypad

For most people, the numeric keypad on a standard keyboard provides little more than a spare set of cursor keys. However, if you enter much numerical data, you might appreciate the convenience of the numeric keypad. So, where is it?

Most notebooks provide a way of using a portion of the alphanumeric keypad as a numeric keypad. You toggle the keypad on and off by pressing and releasing the NumLock key or its equivalent key combination. For example, you might need to hold down the Fn key while pressing one of the function keys. When the numeric keypad is active, the LCD should display that NumLock is on (see Figure 4.3).

Press Fn plus the NumLock or PadLock key.

These keys function as the numeric keypad.

FIGURE 4.3 Notebooks commonly use a portion of the alphanumeric keypad as a numeric keypad.

Typing Characters When NumLock Is On If you want to keep NumLock on but use the keys to type a few characters, hold down the Fn key while typing the desired keys.

Numeric Keypad Disabled   Many notebooks automatically disable the embedded numeric keypad when you connect an external keyboard.

Using the Function Keys

Across the top of the keyboard is a row of function keys labeled F1 to F12. In the days of DOS programs, these keys were essential for entering commands. In Windows programs, however, most of these keys are relatively useless, except for the universal help key: F1. Because of this, most function keys are assigned a specific notebook task, such as adjusting the display's brightness.

To use the function keys to enter commands in Windows or in one of your applications, press the key for the desired command. You can also use the keys in combination with the Ctrl and Shift keys to enter additional commands. Refer to your Windows documentation, the Windows help system, and your application documentation for information about entering commands.

Taking Advantage of the Windows Key

If your keyboard has a key with the Windows logo on it (typically positioned near the lower-left corner of the keyboard), you can use this key to save additional keystrokes (see Table 4.1).

TABLE 4.1 WINDOWS LOGO KEY SHORTCUTS

PRESS	TO
⊞	Open the Start menu.
⊞+Tab	Cycle through open program windows.
⊞+F	Find files or folders.
Ctrl+⊞+F	Find a computer on your company's network.
⊞+F1	Display help for Windows.

PRESS	TO
⊞+R	Display the Run dialog box, which you can use to type the command for running a program.
⊞+Break	Open the System Properties dialog box.
⊞+E	Run Windows Explorer.
⊞+D	Minimize or restore all open program Windows (same as clicking Show/Hide Desktop in the Quick Launch toolbar).
Shift+⊞+M	Undo Minimize All Windows.

 The Windows Table Key   If your notebook has a Windows key, chances are it has a Windows Table key, as well. The Windows Table key has an icon that looks like a document with a mouse pointer next to it. Press this key to display a pop-up menu for the currently selected object in Windows or in your Windows application.

Using Other Not-So-Common Keys

You already know how to use the arrow keys, the Page Up and Page Down keys, the Ctrl and Alt keys, and other common keys to enter commands and navigate your documents, so you don't need a review. However, there are some less common keys that you might have overlooked on a spacious, full-size keyboard. Table 4.2 lists these less common keys to make you aware of their functions and help you troubleshoot if you press a key by mistake.

TABLE 4.2   SOME LESS COMMON KEYS

PRESS	TO
PrtSc	Send the currently displayed screen to the printer or, in Windows, to the Clipboard.
Scroll Lock	Make the arrow keys push text up and down on the screen one line at a time instead of moving the insertion point. (Scroll Lock works only in applications that support it.)
Pause/Break	Stop your computer from performing the same task over and over again, something that DOS and DOS programs were apt to do. In Windows, this key does little.
Ins	Toggle between Insert and Typeover modes. In Typeover mode, new characters you type replace any existing characters that are in their path. In Insert mode, existing characters move over to make room for the new characters. (Ins functions only in some applications.)

This lesson showed you how to expertly navigate your notebook's compact keyboard and use the special keyboard layout. The next lesson shows you how to master your notebook's built-in pointing device and disable it when you want to use a mouse.

LESSON 5

Dealing with Touchpads and Other Pointing Devices

This lesson shows you how to master your notebook's built-in pointing device and disable it when you want to use a mouse.

To work on any computer, you must be able to point and click. Unfortunately, notebooks lack the space to accommodate a mouse. To overcome the problem, notebook designers have developed all sorts of ingenious devices to emulate a mouse. These devices range from touchy-feely touchpads to eraser-shaped TrackPoint "joysticks" embedded in the keyboard.

Using Your Notebook's Built-In Pointing Device

In order to master your notebook and get any work done, you must be able to navigate using your notebook's pointing device. The following sections show you how to use the most common notebook pointing devices.

Using a Touchpad

A touchpad is the most popular mouse alternative. The pad is pressure sensitive, enabling you to move the pointer simply by sliding your finger across it. To use a touchpad, take the following steps:

1. Slide your finger gently across the pad to move the onscreen pointer (see Figure 5.1).

2. To click an item, tap the pad once or click the button to the left of the pad.

3. To double-click, tap the pad twice in quick succession or quickly click the left button twice.

4. To drag a selected object, take one of the following steps:

Tap the pad twice and hold down your finger on the second tap. Slide your finger to drag the item. (This works only on some touchpads.)

Hold down the button to the left of the pad while sliding your finger across the pad. In most cases, if you hold down the right button to drag, a context menu pops up when you release the button.

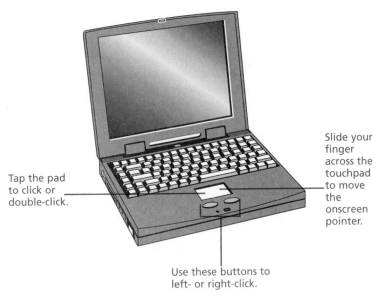

Tap the pad to click or double-click.

Slide your finger across the touchpad to move the onscreen pointer.

Use these buttons to left- or right-click.

FIGURE 5.1   A touchpad provides an intuitive alternative to a mouse.

Dry Your Fingers   Touchpads are very sensitive to both pressure and heat. If your fingers are even slightly moist from perspiration, the onscreen pointer moves erratically. Dry your fingers and gently wipe off the touchpad.

Many touchpads offer additional features that you might not know about without dipping into the documentation or help system. Try the following moves:

- Slide your finger up and down the right edge of the touchpad to scroll documents up and down.

- Slide your finger along the bottom edge of the touchpad to scroll left or right.

- When you reach the edge of the touchpad when scrolling, instead of lifting your finger, keep it on the pad for continuous scrolling. This saves you from having to lift your finger and start from the top.

- Tap the upper-left corner of the touchpad to left-click and the upper-right corner to right-click.

- Try to move the mouse pointer out of the currently active window. If the pointer seems stuck at the edge, your touchpad might have an EdgeFinder feature. This makes it easy to perform common tasks, such as closing or resizing windows, because it stops the pointer at the edge or corner of the window where the required controls are positioned.

Check Your Touchpad Settings   You might need to activate special touchpad features before you can use them. See "Adjusting Your Touchpad's Sensitivity" later in this lesson for instructions on how to access the touchpad's settings.

Using a Trackball

A trackball is like an upside-down mouse. Instead of sliding a mouse to roll the ball beneath it, you roll the ball directly. To use a trackball, take the following steps:

1. Roll the ball to move the onscreen pointer in the desired direction (see Figure 5.2).

2. To click an item, press and release the button to the left of the ball.

3. To double-click, press and release the button to the left of the ball twice in quick succession.

4. To drag a selected object, hold down the button to the left of the ball while rolling the ball in the direction in which you want the object dropped. Release the button.

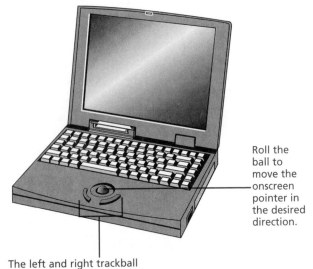

Roll the ball to move the onscreen pointer in the desired direction.

The left and right trackball buttons act just like mouse buttons.

FIGURE 5.2   A trackball is like a mouse flipped on its back.

Using a TrackPoint or AccuPoint Pointer

TrackPoint is IBM's mouse alternative. It consists of a small, red "stick" located smack dab in the middle of the keyboard along with two TrackPoint buttons at the base of the keyboard. This places the pointing device right at your fingertips so that you don't have to move your fingers from the keyboard to point and click. Toshiba's AccuPoint is similar, but differs in two ways: The stick is green and the two "mouse" buttons are arranged vertically, the larger button playing the role of the left mouse button.

To use a TrackPoint or AccuPoint pointer, take the following steps:

1. Push the TrackPoint or AccuPoint stick in the direction in which you want the onscreen pointer to travel (see Figure 5.3).

2. To click an item, press and release the left TrackPoint button (or the larger of the two AccuPoint buttons).

3. To double-click, press and release the left TrackPoint button (or the larger AccuPoint button) twice in quick succession.

4. To drag a selected object, hold down the left TrackPoint button (or the larger AccuPoint button) while pushing the stick in the direction you want to move the object. Release the button.

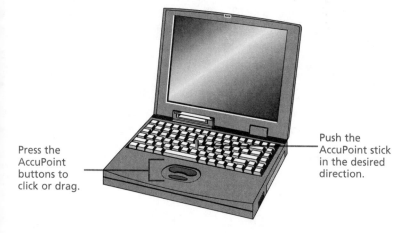

Press the AccuPoint buttons to click or drag.

Push the AccuPoint stick in the desired direction.

FIGURE 5.3   The AccuPoint works like a miniature joystick.

Configuring Your Pointing Device

Instead of letting your notebook's pointing device control you, you can seize control of the pointing device by changing its settings in Windows. The Windows Control Panel features a utility for controlling the speed at which the mouse pointer travels across the screen and the speed at which you must click twice to double-click. If your notebook is equipped with a touchpad, the notebook should also include a utility for setting its sensitivity. The following sections show you how to proceed.

Adjusting the Pointer Speed and Double-Click Interval

As you work, you might notice that the mouse pointer travels too quickly or too slowly across the screen. In addition, you might find that you just can't click fast enough to execute a double-click. To change the pointer speed and double-click interval, take the following steps:

1. Open the Windows Start menu, point to Settings, and click Control Panel.

2. Double-click the Mouse icon. The Mouse Properties dialog box appears.

3. To change the speed at which you must click twice for a double-click, drag the Double-Click Speed slider to the left or right. You can double-click the jack-in-the-box to determine whether you like the new setting.

4. Click the Motion tab, as shown in Figure 5.4.

5. Drag the Pointer Speed slider to the left to decrease the speed of the pointer or to the right to increase its speed.

6. Change any other mouse settings as desired and click OK. (The Pointers tab lets you control the appearance of the mouse pointer.)

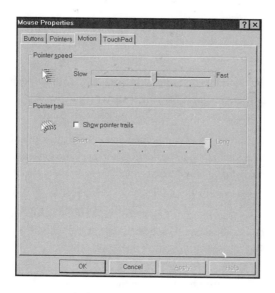

FIGURE 5.4   Take control of your pointing device by changing the mouse properties.

    Disappearing Mouse Pointer?   On notebook displays, the mouse pointer might travel so quickly that it disappears for an instant, making it difficult for you to track its position. To make the pointer more noticeable, turn on Show pointer trails.

Adjusting Your Touchpad's Sensitivity

Although a touchpad is the most popular alternative to a mouse, it can be infuriating to control. A slight touch of the pad can send the pointer scurrying across the screen or select a command you had no intention of executing. To make your touchpad more manageable, try adjusting its sensitivity.

The steps for adjusting the touchpad's sensitivity vary depending on your notebook. Check your documentation or try one of the following steps:

- Open the Windows Control Panel and look for a touchpad or similar icon. If you find a touchpad icon, you're in luck. Double-click the icon to access your touchpad's settings.

- Look on the right end of the Windows taskbar (the system tray) for a touchpad icon. If the icon is there, double-click it. This should bring up a dialog box for adjusting the settings.

- Open the Windows Control Panel and double-click the Mouse icon. The Mouse Properties dialog box appears. On some notebooks, this dialog box has a tab for setting the touchpad properties, as shown in Figure 5.5.

- Check the Start/Programs menu for set of utilities for your notebook or touchpad. Some notebook manufacturers have their own control panel for entering notebook settings.

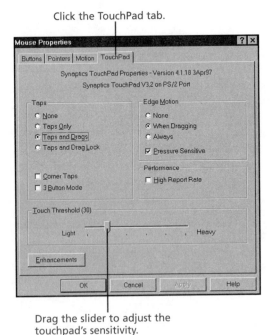

Click the TouchPad tab.

Drag the slider to adjust the touchpad's sensitivity.

FIGURE 5.5   You can adjust your touchpad's sensitivity to make it more manageable.

Download the Latest Touchpad Driver   For optimum control of your touchpad, visit the notebook manufacturer's Web site and copy the latest touchpad driver. A new driver can provide your touchpad with additional features and even some toys, such as the Synaptics MoodPad and Pressure Graph. See Appendix C, "Notebook Tech Support Contact Information," for a list of popular notebook manufacturers' Web sites.

Turning on Single-Click Access in Windows 98

Although this book doesn't focus on Windows basics, Windows does have several features that can make notebook computing much more efficient. If you have Windows 95 with Internet Explorer 4 or Windows 98, you can turn on Web Style, which provides single-click access to programs and documents—you click an icon only once to run a program or open a document. To turn on Web Style, take the following steps:

1. On the Windows desktop, double-click My Computer.

2. Open the View menu and click Folder Options. The Folder Options dialog box appears, as shown in Figure 5.6.

3. Click Web Style.

4. Click OK. In Web Style, icon names appear underlined.

Return to Double-Click Access   If you prefer double-click access to files, open the View menu in My Computer, click Folder Options, click Classic Style, and then click OK.

If icon names are not underlined and you cannot access them with a single click, View as Web Page might be turned off for the desktop or the folder you are currently using. Take one of the following steps:

- In My Computer, display the contents of the desired folder. Open the View menu and click As Web Page.

- Right-click a blank area on the Windows desktop, point to Active Desktop, and click View as Web Page.

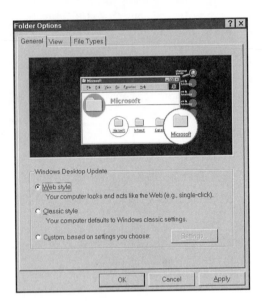

FIGURE 5.6 Turn on Web Style for single-click access to documents, folders, and files.

Disabling the Notebook's Pointing Device

On most notebooks, the touchpad is positioned right below your thumbs, making it easy to brush over the touchpad when you're typing and perform unintentional mouse moves. Decreasing the touchpad's sensitivity rarely solves the problem. If you attach a mouse to your notebook (see Lesson 2, "Connecting Additional Equipment and Devices"), you can disable the touchpad in Windows by taking the following steps:

1. Alt+ click My Computer.

2. Click the Device Manager tab.

3. Click the plus sign next to Mouse.

4. Click the icon for your touchpad driver.

5. Click the Properties button.

6. Click Disable in This Hardware Profile (see Figure 5.7).

7. Click OK.

8. Shut down and restart Windows.

 Using Two Devices   Most notebooks allow you to use both the built-in pointing device and a mouse. You need not disable the pointing device when you install a mouse.

Click
Disable in
This
Hardware
Profile.

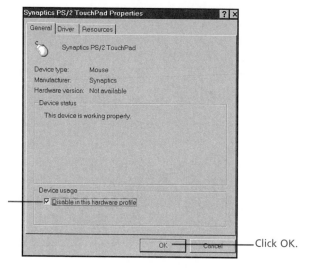

Click OK.

FIGURE 5.7   If you attach a mouse to your notebook, consider disabling your touchpad.

If the touchpad is still active, you might need to disable it in your notebook's setup program. See Lesson 22, "Checking Your Notebook's BIOS Settings," to learn how to access your notebook's system settings.

Hardware Profile Instructions that tell Windows which hardware devices to use. You can create two or more hardware profiles in Windows. For example, a hardware profile for using the notebook in your office might load drivers for a mouse, monitor, and external disk drive, whereas the profile for using the notebook on the road might disable these devices. At startup, Windows prompts you to select the profile you want to load. See Lesson 10, "Plugging into a Docking Station or Port Replicator," for details.

This lesson showed you how to use your notebook's built-in pointing device, configure it, and disable it when it gets in the way. The next lesson shows you how to configure the notebook's display and use an external monitor.

LESSON 6

Changing Your Notebook's Display Settings

This lesson shows you how to take control of your notebook screen's appearance and use an external monitor.

Although you're stuck with the screen that's permanently attached to your notebook, you can configure the display in Windows to increase your work area and make the text more readable. In addition, when you're using your desktop in your home or office, you can attach a standard monitor to make your notebook act more like a desktop PC. This lesson shows you just what to do.

Adjusting the Brightness and Contrast

The easiest way to adjust your notebook's display is to use the brightness and contrast controls built into the notebook. These adjustments are similar to those used on a TV set, but the controls might differ:

- Most notebooks use Fn+key combinations to adjust the brightness and contrast. For example, you might hold down the Fn key while tapping the F1 key to decrease brightness. See Lesson 4, "Navigating the Streamlined Keyboard," for details.

- Some notebooks have built-in slide controls or knobs. Move the slider or turn one of the knobs to adjust the brightness and contrast.

Accessing the Windows Display Settings

To change any of the settings for your notebook's display, use the Display Properties dialog box in Windows. Take the following steps:

1. Right-click a blank area on the Windows desktop.

2. Click Properties. The Display Properties dialog box appears, as shown in Figure 6.1. The appearance of the dialog box and some of its options can vary depending on the version of Windows you use.

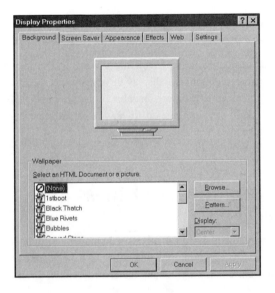

FIGURE 6.1   The Display Properties dialog box provides access to all screen settings.

Your notebook might have a special utility for controlling the display. Check the Start, Programs menu. In some cases, you can access the settings by double-clicking the display's icon in the Windows system tray (at the right end of the taskbar).

Don't Adjust the Screen Refresh Rate The screen refresh rate controls the frequency at which the magic light gun behind the screen re-energizes the glowing dots that make up the display. Increasing the refresh rate to a point at which the monitor can't keep up can damage the monitor.

Adjusting the Resolution and Colors

You can change the display's resolution to increase or decrease the size of objects onscreen. You might be able to fit more on the screen by changing to a higher resolution, for example, from 640×480 to 800×600. You can also decrease the number of colors your monitor uses in order to save memory or increase the number for optimum graphics.

Resolution The number of *pixels* (dots) used to display an image. In general, higher resolution displays produce sharper images and text.

Write Down Your Display's Maximum Resolution Check your documentation to determine the maximum resolution of your display and write it down. On a high-resolution display, you can safely choose lower resolution settings, but choosing a higher resolution than your display supports can make the screen unreadable. If you do enter settings that cause the screen to go blank, Windows will start in Safe mode, enabling you to enter the original settings.

To change screen color and resolution settings, take the following steps:

1. In the Display Properties dialog box, click the Settings tab (see Figure 6.2).

2. Open the Colors drop-down list and click the desired number of colors; 256 is sufficient for most graphics.

3. Under Screen Area, drag the slider to the left to decrease resolution (make objects appear larger) or to the right to increase resolution (fit more on the screen).

4. Click OK.

Choose the desired number of colors.

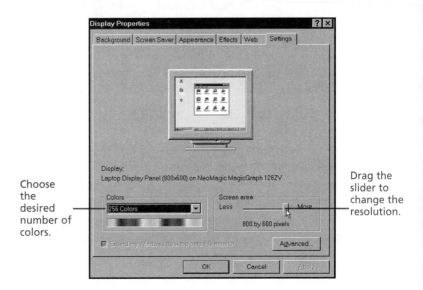

Drag the slider to change the resolution.

FIGURE 6.2   Choose the desired number of colors and set the screen resolution.

   Higher Resolution Unavailable?   If you know that your display supports higher resolutions but the Screen Area slider won't budge, you might have the wrong monitor or display driver installed. See "Changing Display Drivers" later in this lesson for instructions.

Changing the Icon and Font Sizes

If you entered a high-resolution setting for improved graphics, but the text on menus and icons is too small to read, you can choose to display larger icons and text. Take the following steps:

1. In the Display Properties dialog box, click the Settings tab.

2. If the Settings tab does not have a Font Size drop-down list, click the Advanced button. (The steps might vary depending on your version of Windows and on the display adapter your notebook uses.)

3. Open the Font Size drop-down list and choose Large Fonts (for bigger text) or Small Fonts (for smaller text). See Figure 6.3.

4. If you clicked the Advanced button in step 2, click OK now to close the Advanced dialog box.

5. If you're running Windows 98, click the Effects tab to change the icon size.

6. Under Visual Effects, click Use Large icons to place a check in its box.

7. If prompted to restart your computer, save any open documents, close all programs, and click Yes.

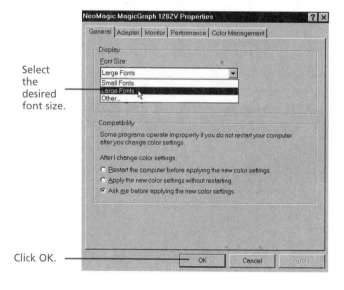

FIGURE 6.3 When displaying higher resolutions, consider increasing the font size.

Controlling the Desktop Colors

Notebook displays, especially liquid-crystal displays, can be difficult to view at certain angles. You might be able to increase the contrast by selecting different colors for the various objects and text that make up the display. Take the following steps:

1. In the Display Properties dialog box, click the Appearance tab (see Figure 6.4).

2. Open the Scheme drop-down list and click the desired color scheme. The preview area displays a sample of the color scheme in action. Try several schemes until you find a scheme that's close to what you want.

3. Open the Item drop-down list and click the name of the object whose color you want to change or click the object in the preview area.

4. Open the Color drop-down list and click the desired color.

5. If the Size option is available, use the Size spin box to set the desired size.

6. If the object contains text, specify the desired font, size, and color of the text.

7. Repeat steps 3 to 6 to change the properties of additional objects.

8. Click OK.

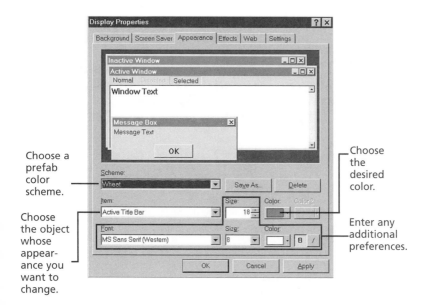

Choose a prefab color scheme.

Choose the object whose appearance you want to change.

Choose the desired color.

Enter any additional preferences.

FIGURE 6.4 Choose colors that help the text stand out against the background.

Changing Display Drivers

Two components contribute to creating a display: the display adapter and the monitor. The display adapter consists of circuitry inside the notebook that sends data to the monitor. The monitor receives data from the display adapter and creates an image onscreen. In order for this display system to work properly, Windows must use the proper device driver for the adapter and the monitor. The following sections show you how to check these device drivers and change them if needed.

If It Ain't Broke, Don't Fix It If your notebook display is working properly, don't change display adapters. Choosing the wrong adapter can blank the screen. If you do choose the wrong adapter, Windows will start in Safe mode, enabling you to change back to the original adapter.

> **Get the Latest Video Driver** PC manufacturers commonly post updated video drivers on their Web sites. If you don't have an Internet connection, call the manufacturer's technical support department and see if you can get the driver on a disk or CD.

Choosing the Correct Display Adapter

If you received an updated display driver from the notebook manufacturer, you might be able to install it by running the downloaded file or inserting the disk and running the setup routine. In most cases, however, you must take the following steps to change device drivers:

1. In the Display Settings dialog box, click the Settings tab.

2. Click the Advanced button.

3. Click the Adapter tab. Information about the currently selected adapter appears below Adapter/Driver Information. Write down this information.

4. Click the Change button. The Update Device Driver Wizard dialog box appears.

5. Click Next. The Wizard asks if you want to search for a better driver or display a list of all drivers.

6. Click Display a list of all the drivers... and click Next. The Wizard prompts you to select your display adapter.

> **Installing from a Disk or Downloaded File** If you have a driver disk from the manufacturer or a downloaded file, click the Have Disk button in step 6 and follow the onscreen instructions to install the driver.

7. Click Show All Hardware. Windows displays a list of all the adapters it supports, as shown in Figure 6.5.

8. Click the company's name in the Manufacturer's list or click (Standard display types).

9. Click the model name and number in the Models list.

10. Click Next and follow the onscreen instructions to complete the setup.

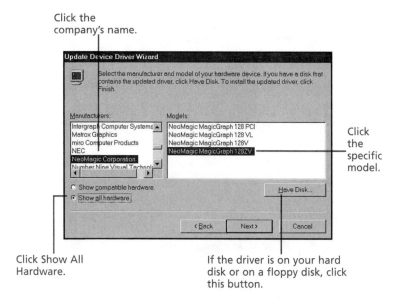

Click the company's name.

Click the specific model.

Click Show All Hardware.

If the driver is on your hard disk or on a floppy disk, click this button.

FIGURE 6.5   Choose the correct display adapter for your notebook.

Choosing the Correct Monitor

When selecting a monitor, choose only the type specified by your manufacturer or one of the Windows standard laptop types. To check the monitor type (and change it if necessary), take the following steps:

1. In the Display Settings dialog box, click the Settings tab.

2. Click the Advanced button.

3. Click the Monitor tab. The currently selected monitor type appears near the top of the tab. Write down its name in case you decide to change back to it later.

4. Click the Change button. The Update Device Driver Wizard dialog box appears.

5. Click Next. The Wizard asks if you want to search for a better driver or display a list of all drivers.

6. Click Display a list of all the drivers… and click Next. The Wizard prompts you to select your monitor.

7. Click Show All Hardware. Windows displays a list of all the displays it supports, as shown in Figure 6.6.

8. Click the name of the notebook display's manufacturer in the Manufacturer's list or click (Standard monitor types).

9. Click the model name and number in the Models list. If you chose (Standard monitor types) in step 8, the top three Laptop Display Panel options work for most displays.

10. Click Next and follow the onscreen instructions to complete the setup.

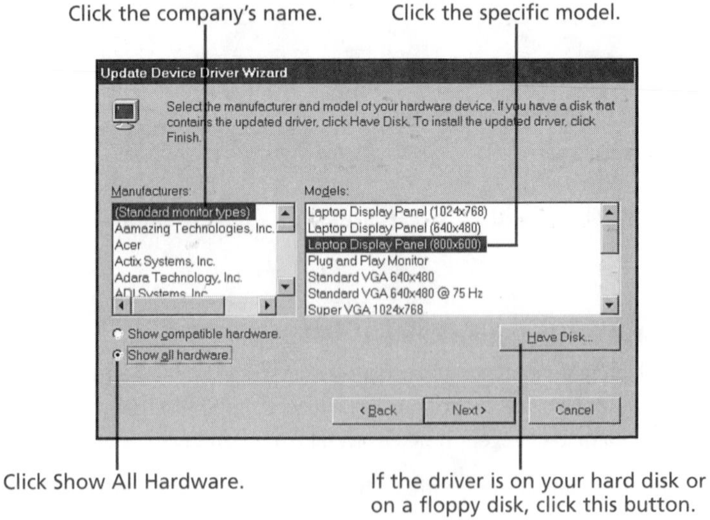

Click the company's name.   Click the specific model.

Click Show All Hardware.   If the driver is on your hard disk or
                                on a floppy disk, click this button.

Figure 6.6 Choose the correct monitor for your notebook.

Use a TV Screen   You can use a TV as your monitor, although the picture might be a little blurry. In step 8, click (Standard monitor types) and then scroll to the bottom of the Models list and click Television. (This option might not be available if your notebook is running an early version of Windows.) If you do use a TV as your monitor, change the display resolution to 640 × 480. Standard TVs do not support high-resolution output.

Setting Up an External Monitor

As discussed in Lesson 2, most notebooks have a VGA port for connecting an external monitor. To connect the monitor and set up your notebook to use it, take the following steps:

1. Make sure the monitor and notebook are off.

2. Place the monitor on the desk next to your notebook. Never place the monitor on top of your notebook.

3. Plug the VGA connector on the monitor into the VGA port on the notebook, as explained in Lesson 2.

4. Plug in the monitor.

5. Turn on the monitor and then turn on your notebook. Windows senses that a new monitor has been connected and leads you through the process of installing the display driver. (If Windows does not prompt you to install a new driver and your monitor is blank, open the Windows Control Panel and double-click the Add New Hardware icon.)

6. Follow the onscreen instructions to install the necessary driver from the Windows CD or from the disk that came with the monitor. (Refer to the previous section, "Choosing the Correct Monitor," for details.)

7. If your keyboard has a button or key sequence for switching the output from the notebook display to the monitor, press it. Some

notebooks let you toggle between LCD (notebook) and CRT
(monitor) mode by holding down the Fn key and pressing the
LCD/CRT key. See Lesson 4, "Navigating the Streamlined
Keyboard," for details about the Fn key.

When you take your notebook on the road (and are not using the external
monitor), Windows might display an error message on startup indicating
that it cannot find the monitor. Simply cancel the error message. You can
avoid these error messages by setting up hardware profiles, as discussed
in Lesson 10, "Plugging into a Docking Station or Port Replicator."

 Check Your Display Utility If your notebook has its
own utility for controlling the display, pull it up and
see whether it has a setting for directing the video
output to the VGA port.

 Still No Display? If your notebook does not identify
the monitor and the screen is still blank, your notebook's VGA port might be disabled. Check your
notebook's system settings, as explained in Lesson 22,
"Checking Your Notebook's BIOS Settings," and turn
on the option for using an external monitor.

This lesson showed you how to configure your notebook's display and
connect to a full-size monitor. The next lesson shows you how to make
your notebook run longer on battery power.

LESSON 7
Conserving Battery Power

This lesson shows you how to make your notebook run longer on a single charge.

When you power up your notebook on a battery, the clock starts ticking. If you're lucky, you have about two and a half hours to work (or play) before your system grinds to a halt. A power loss not only prevents you from continuing, but it can improperly shut down your notebook, messing up Windows and causing you to lose data. In this lesson, you learn how to use your battery power more efficiently.

 More Power! Many newer notebooks have a multi-function bay that can hold either a disk drive or a spare battery. With two lithium-ion batteries loaded, your notebook might be able to run for up to six hours on a single charge.

Using the Windows Power-Saving Features

The Windows Power Management utility can double the life of your battery by powering down your monitor and hard disk drive after a specified amount of time. You can even turn on warnings to have Windows notify you when the battery is running down so that you can save your work and shut down Windows before the battery goes dead.

Changing the Power Management Settings

To change any of the Power Management settings in Windows, take the following steps:

1. Open the Control Panel and click the Power Management icon. The Power Management Properties dialog box appears, as shown in Figure 7.1.

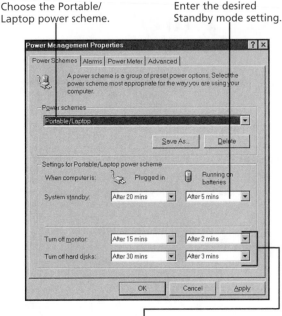

Choose the Portable/
Laptop power scheme.

Enter the desired
Standby mode setting.

Specify how long you want Windows to wait
before shutting down the monitor and hard drive.

FIGURE 7.1 You can enter separate power management settings for when the PC is running on battery power.

2. Open the Power Schemes drop-down list and click Portable/ Laptop.

3. Open the System Standby, Running on Batteries drop-down list and choose the number of minutes of inactivity you want to pass before Windows puts your notebook in Standby mode (turning off the monitor and hard drive but ready to leap into action).

4. Open the Turn Off Monitor drop-down list and choose the number of minutes of inactivity you'll allow to pass before Windows turns off the monitor.

5. Open the Turn Off Hard Disks drop-down list and choose the number of minutes or hours of inactivity you'll allow to pass before Windows turns off the hard drive.

6. Click the Alarms tab. By default, Windows displays a message whenever the battery power level reaches 5 percent and 3 percent. You can drag the sliders to the right to be notified sooner or to the left to be notified later.

7. To change the way Windows notifies you of low battery power, click one of the Alarm Action buttons.

8. In the Low Battery Alarm Actions dialog box, turn on Sound Alarm if you want Windows to sound an alarm when the battery power drops to the specified level.

9. Under Power Level, click When the Alarm Goes Off, the Computer Will, and then open the drop-down list and choose Standby or Shutdown. Standby keeps Windows running but turns off the monitor and hard disk drives.

10. To force your notebook computer to go into Standby or Shutdown mode even if a program is not responding, click Force Standby or Shutdown Even if a Program Stops Responding. (This can cause data loss, however, so you might want to leave this option off.)

11. Click OK.

12. Click the Advanced tab. Show Power Meter on Taskbar is on by default. You should leave this option on so that you can easily see the battery power level in the system tray.

13. To prevent unauthorized use of your computer when it goes off standby, choose Prompt for Password When Computer Goes Off Standby.

14. Click OK.

Save Your Work   Whenever your notebook is going to remain inactive for several minutes, save your work. Windows does not save your work to disk before kicking into Standby mode. If the battery runs down while your notebook is in Standby mode, you will lose any changes you've made to your documents.

Turning on Hibernation Mode

If your computer supports *Hibernation mode*, you can turn on this feature in Windows so that when you press your notebook's power button or close its lid on a notebook PC, Windows saves your work and settings to disk before turning off the power. The next time you turn on your PC, it will jump into action and be ready to use just as you left it.

Hibernation Settings Unavailable?   Not all notebooks support Hibernation mode. If the settings are unavailable in Windows, your notebook does not support the hibernation feature.

To turn on Hibernation mode, take the following steps:

1. In the Windows Control Panel, double-click the Power Management icon.

2. Click the Hibernate tab and click the option for turning on Hibernation mode to place a check in its box.

3. Click the Advanced tab.

4. To make the power button place your notebook in Hibernation mode rather than turning it completely off, click When I Press the Power Button on My Computer and click Hibernate.

5. To make your notebook go into Hibernation mode when you close its lid (instead of turning off), click When I Close the Lid of My Computer and then click Hibernate.

6. Click OK to save your settings.

Hibernation mode actually turns off the power. To restart, you must press and hold the power button for one or two seconds to turn on the power.

Checking the Remaining Battery Power

Your notebook's LCD should display a battery icon showing the remaining battery power. To display the remaining power in Windows, take the following steps:

1. Rest the mouse pointer on the power plug or battery icon in the Windows system tray (on the right end of the taskbar). A ScreenTip appears showing the amount of power remaining.

2. To display additional details, double-click the power plug or battery icon. The Power Meter dialog box appears, as shown in Figure 7.2.

 Power Plug or Battery Icon?   The system tray displays a power plug icon when the AC adapter is connected. When the notebook is running on batteries, the battery icon appears and shows the remaining battery power.

The Power Meter dialog box
provides additional details.

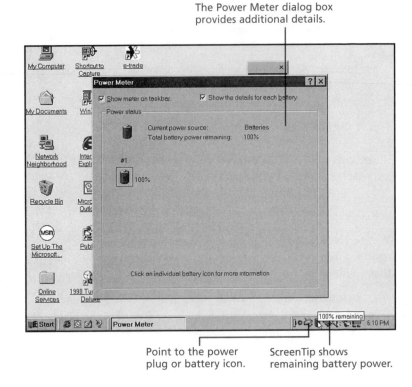

Point to the power   ScreenTip shows
plug or battery icon.   remaining battery power.

FIGURE 7.2   Check your battery power in Windows.

Adjusting the Notebook's Power-Saving Settings

Most notebooks have built-in power-saving features that automatically shut down the power-hungry monitor and hard disk drive, even when Windows is not running. If you usually have Windows running on your notebook, don't mess with the settings for the built-in features. Use the Windows Power Management utility, as described in the previous section.

If you run DOS programs, you can change the built-in power-saving settings via the system setup. Check your notebook documentation to determine which key to press during startup in order to enter the system setup. On some notebooks, you must enter a command at the DOS prompt.

DOS Prompt   DOS (pronounced *DAWSS*) is a non-graphical operating system. The DOS prompt is the operating system's way of asking you to enter a command. It normally appears as **C:\>**.

Watch the Startup Screen   Most notebooks display the key you must press on startup to access the system setup. Typically, you press the F1, F2, or Delete key. Be quick about it; if Windows starts, you miss your opportunity to enter the system setup. If you miss the opportunity to enter system setup, restart Windows and try again.

To change the notebook's built-in power-saving settings, take the following steps:

1. Start your notebook and enter the system setup as explained in the documentation. (See Lesson 22, "Checking Your Notebook's BIOS Settings," for details about changing system settings.)

2. Use the arrow keys to select the Power menu (see Figure 7.3).

3. Press the down arrow key to highlight the setting you want to change.

4. Use the + and - keys to change the setting. If a feature is set to Off, pressing + turns it on. If a feature is set to shut down a device after a specified number of minutes, + increases the time and - decreases it. With some system setup menus, you highlight the field and press Enter to display a pop-up menu containing the available options; highlight the desired option and press Enter.

5. Press Esc to return to the main menu.

6. Use the arrow keys to highlight the command for saving your changes and exiting and then press Enter.

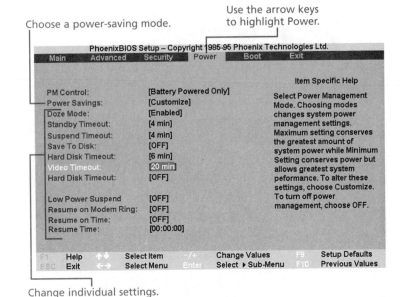

Choose a power-saving mode.

Use the arrow keys
to highlight Power.

Change individual settings.

FIGURE 7.3   Enter your power preferences in system setup.

Suspending Operations Manually

Although the power-saving features kick in automatically, you can trigger
them manually. The easiest way to power down your notebook without
turning it off is to press Fn+Suspend or Fn+Standby key combination.
(See Lesson 4, "Navigating the Streamlined Keyboard," for details about
the Fn key.) When you're ready to start working again, press the Shift key
or another innocuous keystroke to rouse your notebook.

Close the Lid   You can put some systems into
power-saving mode by closing the lid, but check your
documentation before doing this. Many notebooks
shut down completely when the lid is closed, which
can cause data loss.

In Windows, take the following steps to place your notebook in Standby mode:

1. Save any open documents to prevent losing data if the power goes out in Standby mode. Windows does not save your work to disk before going on standby.

2. Click the Start button and click Shut Down.

3. Click Stand by and click OK, as shown in Figure 7.4. Your screen goes blank and your notebook might beep. The LCD panel should display an icon indicating that your notebook is in Sleep mode.

4. When you're ready to start working, press the Shift key.

Click OK.   Click Stand by.

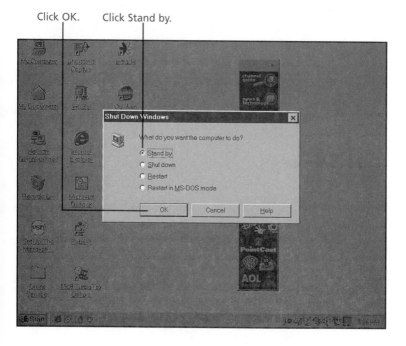

FIGURE 7.4   Shut down in Standby mode.

Power-Conservation Tips

A power-saving utility can make your notebook run nearly twice as long on a single charge. The following list provides additional tips to make your notebook run even longer:

- Run your PC from the AC adapter whenever possible.

- Don't play audio CDs while you're working.

- Disconnect any USB devices when you're not using them.

- If you're not using a PC card that's installed, eject it. See Lesson 8, "Inserting and Removing PC (PCMCIA) Cards."

- Work at room temperature. Batteries lose their charge faster when they're cold.

- Refresh your battery by letting it run down completely and then fully recharging it. This ensures that the battery receives a full charge.

This lesson showed you how to conserve battery power. The next lesson provides instructions for safely inserting and ejecting PC cards.

LESSON 8

Inserting and Removing PC (PCMCIA) Cards

This lesson introduces you to the PC Card Bus and shows you how to safely insert and eject PC cards.

If you ever installed an expansion board in a desktop PC, you know how inconvenient it is to upgrade a desktop PC. You must remove the cover from your system unit, remove the cover plate at the back of the PC, install the board, and then put everything back together again. And if the board conflicts with other devices on your PC, you must flip the hood again and use jumpers or switches to change the card's settings or fiddle with software settings.

Most notebooks make it much easier to upgrade by using *PCMCIA cards* (*PC cards*, for short). These cards are about the size of credit cards, and you typically insert them when the power is on.

 Expansion Board   A printed circuit board that adds capabilities to a computer. For example, you might install an expansion board to add a modem, improve audio output, soup up your display, or add a TV tuner. PC cards are mini-expansion boards that are much easier to install.

Expanding Your Notebook's Capabilities with PC Cards

PC cards enable you to significantly expand the capabilities of your notebook. You simply insert the PC card into one of the PC slots on your notebook, just as if you were inserting a floppy disk. The following list provides a sample of the components and devices you can add with PC cards:

- **Modem**   A PC card modem typically has a phone jack or a phone-jack cable that enables you to connect your modem to a phone line. Some PC card modems are specially designed to connect to cellular phone service.

- **Network adapter**   A network adapter enables you to connect your notebook to another computer or to a network server to share data and resources with other computers.

- **Hard drive**   If your notebook does not enable you to install a second hard drive, your can add a drive with a PC card.

- **Memory**   Memory cards provide a quick way to add random access memory (RAM) to your notebook without having to open the case.

- **Joystick**   Most notebooks don't include a joystick (game) port. To play your favorite video game with a joystick, use a PC card to add the port.

- **USB**   If you have an older notebook, it might not have a USB port. To take advantage of the convenience and expandability of USB, add the ports with a PC card. You might also want to use a USB PC card adapter to install additional USB ports.

- **CD-ROM, DVD, or floppy drive**   Some notebooks skimp on drives. However, you can add just about any type of external drive you want by using a PC card.

- **Video capture or TV tuner**   Although many newer notebooks can output video to a TV, VCR, or projector, few have a video input port. With a video capture card, your notebook can pull in video from a camera or camcorder so that you can teleconference or edit video clips. With a TV tuner card, you can connect your notebook to a cable or standard antenna and watch TV.

- **Global Positioning Systems (GPS)**   A GPS device enables your notebook to receive satellite input to pinpoint your location on the globe. You can use such a system in your car to navigate the highways. See Lesson 18, "Navigating the Highways Via Satellite."

Smart Shopping Tip   Some PC cards have a port or jack directly attached to the card. Although this might seem like an ingenious idea, a large jack or port can block access to the other PC card slot, making it difficult to insert and eject cards. In many cases, you're better off using a standard card that uses a PC card cable.

Understanding PCMCIA and CardBus Standards

PCMCIA (Personal Computer Memory Card International Association) is a group of over 500 companies that has developed standards for PC cards. The PCMCIA standard controls the design of PC cards to ensure notebook compatibility. CardBus, developed in 1995, is a 32-bit version of the PCMCIA standard. CardBus PC card slots are standard issue on newer notebooks (those manufactured in 1996 and later years).

When you're shopping for or using PC cards, you should understand the basic advantages of CardBus over standard PCMCIA:

- **32-bit bus**   A bus is a data highway. CardBus features a 32-bit bus, which is twice as wide as the standard PCMCIA bus. This increases the amount of data that the card can transfer to the notebook in a single instant.

- **33MHz communications**   In addition to having a wider bus, CardBus supports higher communications speeds that are 20 times faster than the old PCMCIA standard.

- **Multi-function card support**   A CardBus PC card can perform more than one function; for example, one card can act as both a fax modem and a network adapter. A standard PCMCIA card can handle only one job.

- **Bus mastering**   This technology enables two devices to communicate with each other without having to go through the processor. For instance, a video capture card can send the audio portion of the video directly to the sound card. This frees the processor to perform other tasks it is better suited to perform.

- **Power-saving**   CardBus PC card slots use less power than their PCMCIA siblings. CardBus PC cards are designed for 3.3V instead of 5V, enabling them to function on less power. In addition, the notebook automatically turns off power to a CardBus slot when the card is ejected or has remained inactive for a specified period.

 Compatibility Issues   If your notebook does not support the CardBus standard, a CardBus card will not function properly. However, you can use older PCMCIA cards in slots that support the CardBus standard.

Understanding PC Card Types

When you are shopping for a PC card, you should keep in mind that there are three types of cards. They are all the same length and width, but their thickness varies:

- Type I cards (the thinnest of the bunch) are almost exclusively used to add notebook memory or flash memory that acts as a hard drive. A flash card is a cross between memory and disk storage. It is fast, like RAM chips, but unlike RAM chips, flash cards store data even when the power is off.

- Type II cards (up to 5.5 mm thick) are typically used to add a fax modem, network adapter, or external disk or CD-ROM drive (the drive can be connected to the PCMCIA card with a cable or directly plugged into the card). Type II cards are the most common.

- Type III cards (the thickest of the bunch) are usually used for adding an internal hard disk drive. A Type III card uses the entire slot, leaving no room for additional cards.

Your notebook computer should have one or more PC card slots. These slots also come in three types:

- Type I slots can hold only one Type I card. A Type I slot cannot house a Type II or Type III card.

- Type II slots can hold two Type I cards or one Type II card.

- Type III slots can hold one Type III card or one Type I card and one Type II card.

Inserting a PC Card

Because Windows supports Plug and Play PC cards, you can swap cards in and out of the slots without turning off your notebook and without having to worry about setting jumpers or DIP switches to prevent hardware conflicts. However, if your notebook does not support PC card hot plugging, you might need to turn off your notebook before inserting or removing cards.

Hot Plugging Ideally, you should be able to insert and remove PC cards without having to turn off your notebook or restart it. This is called *hot plugging* or *hot swapping*. However, some older PC cards and notebooks don't support the latest PC card standards, which enable hot plugging. To avoid damaging your notebook or PC card, check the manufacturer's documentation to determine whether it is safe to exchange cards while your system is running.

Remove Any Spacers from the Slots   The manufacturer might have inserted plastic or cardboard spacers in the PC card slots to protect them during shipping. Before inserting a card, eject the spacers. Eject mechanisms on notebooks vary. On most notebooks, you press a button next to the slot two times; the first press typically makes the button pop out, and the second press makes the spacer pop out. Other notebooks use a sliding lever to eject cards. Notebooks that have two card slots typically use a separate eject mechanism for each slot.

To insert a PC card into one of the PC slots on your notebook, take the following steps:

1. Insert the PC card (label up) into one of the PC card slots on your notebook (see Figure 8.1). The card should be firmly seated in the slot, but don't force it. Windows sounds a two-tone beep (a medium tone followed by a high tone) to indicate that it has identified and activated the card. If this is the first time you've inserted the card, Windows runs the Add New Hardware Wizard.

First Slot First   If you have two empty slots, typically marked 0 and 1, use the number 0 (top) slot first.

2. Click Next. The wizard asks if you want to search for the best driver for the device or display the drivers on a specific disk.

3. Click Search for the Best Driver for Your Device and click Next. The wizard displays a list of all the locations it will search.

4. If the device came with an installation disk or CD, insert it into the floppy disk drive or CD-ROM drive and click Floppy Disk Drives and CD-ROM Drive (see Figure 8.2).

FIGURE 8.1   Insert the PC card into the PC card slot and push it in gently but firmly.

FIGURE 8.2   Windows can search your drives for the best device driver.

Windows 98 Update   In Windows 98, you can click the Microsoft Windows Update option to check Microsoft's Web site for updated drivers. If you have not yet registered your copy of Windows 98, the Microsoft Windows Update option will be unavailable (grayed out).

5. Click Next. The wizard locates the required driver and displays its name.

6. Click Next.

7. The wizard displays a message indicating that it has successfully installed the driver. Click Finish.

8. If the card requires you to connect a cable, phone line, or other device, plug the cable or phone line into the opening on the card.

9. If you are connecting an external device that requires power, plug in the device's power cable and turn on the device, if necessary.

Ejecting a PC Card

Because PC cards enable you to add devices on-the-fly, you can eject one card and replace it with another to use a different device. However, before ejecting a card, you should disable it in Windows. This unloads the driver and shuts the power off to the PC card slot. To properly eject a PC card, take the following steps:

1. Click the PC Card (PCMCIA) Status icon in the system tray and then click the Stop... option for the card you want to remove (see Figure 8.3). A dialog box appears indicating that it is safe to remove the card.

2. Click OK.

3. Eject the PC card. (This step varies depending on the eject mechanism your notebook uses.) The card pops out of the slot and Windows emits a two-toned beep (a high tone followed by a medium tone).

4. Pull the card out of the slot.

 Turn Off Your Notebook?   If your notebook does not support hot plugging, shut down Windows and turn off your notebook before ejecting the card. Do not take the preceding steps.

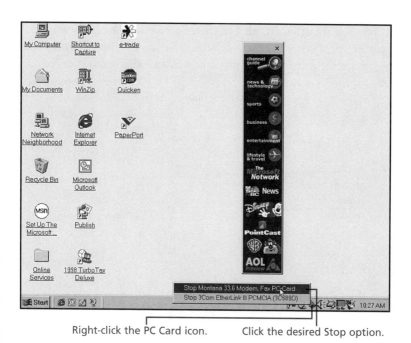

Right-click the PC Card icon.   Click the desired Stop option.

FIGURE 8.3   Before you eject a PC card, you should disable it in Windows.

Save Power   Some PC cards use power even while inactive. If you're running on battery power and are not using the card, eject it.

Keep the Card in Its Case   When you're not using the PC card, keep it in its protective case to prevent damaging the contacts. If your notebook came with spacers, you might need to insert the spacers to protect the contacts in your notebook.

This lesson taught you PC card basics and showed you how to insert and eject PC cards safely. The next lesson provides instructions for setting up wireless connections between your notebook and other infrared devices using the IrDA port.

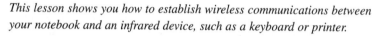

LESSON 9

Communi-cating with Infrared (Wireless) Devices

This lesson shows you how to establish wireless communications between your notebook and an infrared device, such as a keyboard or printer.

Most notebooks have a built-in infrared (IrDA) port, which supports cable-free (wireless) connections. With an infrared port, your notebook can connect to an infrared network adapter, printer, mouse, keyboard, and other accessories that support infrared communications.

 IrDA Short for *Infrared Data Association*, *IrDA* is a group that defines the standards for infrared data communications.

 Infrared Infrared is light that is beyond red in the color spectrum. It is invisible to the human eye.

The Pros and Cons of Infrared Technology

Nearly every notebook on the market has an infrared port. The reason these ports have become standard fare on notebooks is that they offer several advantages over cable connections:

Convenience   With an infrared port, you can set your notebook in front of your printer and start printing. You don't need to disconnect the printer cable from your desktop computer to connect it to your notebook or fumble with network cables to connect two computers.

Elimination of tangled cables   Because infrared devices are wireless, you have no cables to untangle, at least in theory. Actually, many infrared adapters have two cables: one to supply power to the adapter and another for the receiver. The cable for the receiver helps you align it with the infrared light from your notebook.

Fast communications   Standard infrared ports and devices communicate at nearly the same speed as a serial port, which is pretty slow. Fast infrared (FIr) devices communicate at up to 4Mbps (megabits per second), which is pretty fast, but your notebook must support FIr.

Hot swapping   Because there are no cables to attach, you can swap one device with another without turning off your notebook or the device you are connecting to.

Security   Infrared light cannot travel through walls, so no one can eavesdrop on you. Wireless devices that communicate using radio frequency signals provide less security because the signals can travel through walls.

If you pace the aisles of your neighborhood computer store, you won't find many infrared devices on the shelves. You might find a wireless keyboard, a portable printer, and maybe even an cordless mouse, but many such devices use radio frequency signals instead of infrared light. So why are infrared devices so scarce? Because they have some significant drawbacks:

Direct line of sight required   You must point your notebook's infrared port right at the infrared receiver on the other device to establish communications. Given the fact that the infrared port is typically located at the back of a notebook, aligning the port with an infrared receiver can be difficult.

Short-range communications   Your notebook's infrared port must be no more than three to nine feet from the infrared port on the device you want to use. Most manufacturers suggest a distance of one to three feet.

Slow relative speed   A USB port can transfer data more reliably at 12Mbps, three times the speed as a fast infrared port. Older SIr (Serial Infrared) ports transfer data at a maximum speed of 115KBps (kilobytes per second).

Interference   If two or more IrDA systems are in the same room, the systems can interfere with one another, causing *crosstalk* and resulting in miscommunication between devices.

More Information   For details about IrDA, check out www.irda.org/use/. You'll find a list of commonly asked questions and answers, a description of how the technology works, and links to IrDA device manufacturers.

Locating the Infrared Port on Your Notebook

Most notebook owners I've talked to don't even know their notebooks have an infrared port until I point it out to them. The port is typically located at the back of the notebook and is covered by translucent plastic (typically red). The port should be marked IR or IrDA (see Figure 9.1). It's important to know where the port is so that you can point it directly at your other infrared device.

Keep It Clean   Wipe any dust or other debris from the cover of the infrared port to ensure clear communications.

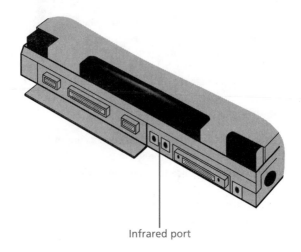

Infrared port

FIGURE 9.1   Find the infrared port on your notebook.

Adding Infrared Capabilities to Your Existing Hardware

Although your notebook probably has an infrared port, most of your existing hardware (including your desktop PC and printer) do not. You can make these devices infrared-ready by installing special adapters.

For about a hundred bucks, you can add an infrared adapter to your printer, as shown in Figure 9.2. A typical infrared printer adapter consists of an infrared receiver with a parallel pass-through port, which enables you to keep the printer connected to your desktop PC while printing from your notebook.

You won't find many infrared adapters at your local computer store, so you'll have to shop through a mail-order company. Here's a list of places to check out:

CMPExpress.com at www.cmpexpress.com or call 800-950-2671.

Chili Pepper Computers at www.chilipepperpc.com or call 877-244-5472.

P.M.I. at www.pmiweb.com or call 619-549-4405.

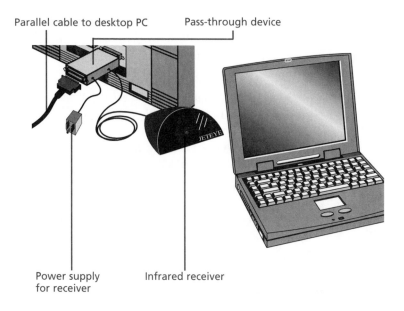

Parallel cable to desktop PC   Pass-through device

Power supply
for receiver   Infrared receiver

FIGURE 9.2   You can add infrared capabilities to your existing
hardware.

    Find It on the Web   If you have an Internet
connection, fire up your Web browser, go to
www.wheretobuy.com, and search for the desired
adapter type. See Appendix A, "Notebook Toys and
Accessories," for additional suggestions.

Installing Your Infrared Port Software

Chances are that your notebook already has the software required to use
the IrDA port. If your notebook is running Windows, open the Control
Panel and check to see whether there is an Infrared icon. If the Control
Panel has an Infrared icon, skip to "Activating the Infrared Port in
Windows."

If the Infrared icon is missing, contact the notebook manufacturer or check its technical support area on the Web. You might need to install special software to use the port. If your notebook manufacturer does not supply the required software, try the following products:

Windows 95 IrDA 2.0   If your notebook is running Windows 95, get the latest IrDA driver from Microsoft's Web site at www.microsoft.com/windows95/downloads/default.asp. The following sections show you how to remove the old IrDA driver (if present) and install the updated IrDA driver.

JetBeam or QuickBeam   JetBeam and QuickBeam are third-party software packages for Windows 3.1, 95, 98, and Windows NT. They are more full-featured than the Windows Infrared Monitor, enabling you to "beam" files from one device to another using drag-and-drop or the Windows Send To feature. For more information, contact CounterPoint Systems Foundry at www.countersys.com or by calling 541-758-6123.

 Windows 98 Infrared Monitor   If the Infrared Monitor is not installed in Windows 98, use the Add New Hardware utility (in the Control Panel) to install the Windows driver for the infrared port.

Removing the Old IrDA Driver in Windows 95

Before you install a new IrDA driver in Windows 95, you should remove the old driver. Take the following steps:

1. If the Infrared Monitor is running, press Ctrl+Alt+Del, click Irmon, and click the End Task button.

2. Click the Start button, point to Settings, and click Control Panel.

3. Double-click the Add/Remove Programs icon and then click the Install/Uninstall tab.

4. Click the name of the IR entry (for example, Infrared Support for Windows...) and then click the Add/Remove button.

5. When prompted to restart the computer, click Yes.

Installing an Updated IrDA Driver in Windows 95

After you remove the old IrDA driver in Windows 95, you can safely install the new driver. Take the following steps:

1. Click the Start button and click Run.

2. Click the Browse button and use the resulting dialog box to change to the folder that contains the Setup.exe file you downloaded or received from the notebook manufacturer.

3. Click the Setup.exe file and then click the Open button.

4. Click OK. The Setup utility copies some files and then starts the Add Infrared Device Wizard.

5. Follow the Wizard's instructions until you are asked to specify the manufacturer and model of your infrared device and then choose (Standard Infrared Devices).

6. Choose the communications port that your notebook has assigned to the infrared port. This is typically COM2.

 Which COM Port Is It? You can determine which COM port your notebook assigns to the infrared port by entering the notebook's system setup, as explained in Lesson 22, "Checking Your Notebook's BIOS Settings." The infrared settings are typically on the Advanced menu. Don't change these settings.

7. Enter any other requested settings and preferences until you reach the last dialog box and then click the Finish button.

Activating the Infrared Port in Windows

When you enable infrared communications in Windows, Windows runs the Infrared Monitor in the background and displays an icon for it in the system tray. The Monitor checks the infrared port regularly to determine whether any infrared devices are within range. It then automatically establishes a connection with the device. To enable the Infrared Monitor, take the following steps:

1. Click or double-click the Infrared Monitor icon on the right end of the status bar (it looks like a tiny red light or two red lights, if an infrared device is in range). The Infrared Monitor dialog box appears.

What About the Control Panel's Infrared Icon? The Infrared icon in the control panel runs the Add Infrared Device Wizard. It does not enable you to change the properties of the Infrared device.

2. Click the Options tab and click Enable infrared communication to place a check in its box (see Figure 9.3).

3. Click Search for And Provide Status for Devices Within Range to place a check in its box.

4. Enter the desired number of seconds to specify how frequently you want Windows to check for new devices.

5. Make sure Install Software for Plug and Play Devices within Range is checked.

6. Click the Preferences tab.

7. Place a check mark next to all three options so that Windows can notify you of the status of your infrared connections.

8. If you are using the infrared port to connect to a network, click the Identification tab and specify your computer and workgroup name. See Lesson 13, "Connecting Your Notebook and Desktop PCs," for more information about networking.

Have Windows check the
port for new devices.

Enable the
Infrared port.

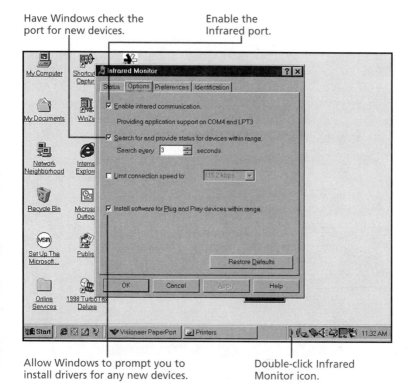

Allow Windows to prompt you to
install drivers for any new devices.

Double-click Infrared
Monitor icon.

FIGURE 9.3   In order to use your infrared port, you must enable infrared communications.

9. Click OK.

10. Right-click the Infrared Monitor icon in the system tray to view the infrared communications options.

Installing Infrared Devices

Most infrared devices are plug-and-play compatible. The first time you connect a plug-and-play device, Windows identifies it and leads you through the process of installing the software required to use it. To install a plug-and-play infrared device, take the following steps:

1. Make sure the Infrared Monitor is running, as explained in the previous section.

2. Turn on the device. (You might need to plug in the device or install batteries before turning it on.)

3. Point your notebook's infrared port in the general direction of the infrared port on the device. The devices should be no farther apart than three to nine feet.

4. If the Add Infrared Device Wizard does not start automatically, open the Control Panel and double-click the Infrared icon (see Figure 9.4).

 Not Too Close, Not Too Far   If Windows does not detect the device, it might be out of range. Try to arrange your notebook and the other device so that they are about two feet apart.

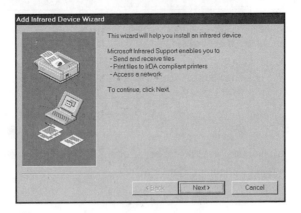

FIGURE 9.4   When the Infrared Monitor detects the infrared device for the first time, it runs the Add Infrared Device Wizard.

5. Follow the Wizard's instructions to install the driver for the device. (You can install the driver from the Windows CD or from a disk or CD that came with the device.)

You might need to install additional software. For example, if you hooked up an infrared receiver to your printer, you must install the printer driver for that printer. Refer to the Windows Help system for instructions on installing a printer.

Is Plug and Play Enabled?   Right-click the Infrared icon on the right end of the taskbar and make sure is checked. If it is not checked, click Enable Plug and Play. If this option is unavailable, check the settings in the Infrared Monitor dialog box.

Deactivating the Infrared Port

When you're not using an infrared device, it's a good idea to disable the Infrared Monitor. This tells Windows to stop checking for devices and prevents the infrared port from consuming power. To disable the Infrared Monitor, take the following steps:

1. Click or double-click the Infrared Monitor icon on the right end of the taskbar. The Infrared Monitor dialog box appears.

2. Click the Options tab and click Enable infrared communication to remove the check from its box.

3. Click OK.

Quick Disable   Right-click the Infrared Monitor icon on the right end of the taskbar and click Enable infrared communications to remove the check from its box.

This lesson introduced you to the infrared port and showed you how to establish a connection between your notebook and another infrared device. The next lesson shows you how to make your notebook look and act more like a desktop PC by plugging it into a docking station.

LESSON 10

Plugging into a Docking Station or Port Replicator

This lesson shows you how to use your notebook as a desktop PC with the help of a docking station or port replicator.

A *docking station* or *port replicator* is a unit that contains ports for a monitor, printer, keyboard, mouse, speakers, and other devices. A docking station can also include drive bays and expansion slots. A docking port (also called an *expansion port*) on the back of the notebook plugs into the docking station, which connects the notebook to the other devices. A docking station enables you to combine the portability of your notebook with the power of a desktop PC.

 No Docking Station or Port Replicator? If you don't have a docking station or port replicator, you can connect external devices to your notebook's built-in ports, as explained in Lesson 2, "Connecting Additional Equipment and Devices." Follow the instructions later in this lesson to create hardware profiles for managing the add-on devices.

 Hardware Profile A hardware profile is a list that tells Windows which devices to use. To avoid conflicts, you can create two hardware profiles: one for when you use the notebook by itself, and another for when the notebook is connected to additional devices.

Docking Station Versus Port Replicator

A docking station offers greater expandability than does a port replicator. In addition to ports for connecting a monitor, keyboard, and mouse, a docking station typically includes drive bays and expansion slots, just like a desktop PC. A port replicator merely provides a convenient way to connect your notebook to several external peripherals rather than connecting the devices individually to the notebook's built-in ports.

 Use the Right Docking Station No standards govern the design of docking stations or port replicators, so use only a docking station or port replicator specifically designed for your notebook. Contact your notebook's manufacturer. Many notebooks go to market long before a docking station or port replicator is available, so you might have to wait.

Plug and Play and Hot Docking

Before you plug your notebook into a docking station or port replicator, check the notebook's documentation to determine whether it supports Plug and Play and hot docking:

- **Plug and Play** Plug and Play enables you to plug your notebook into the docking station and immediately start using the devices connected to the docking station. Windows automatically detects the docking station and all attached devices and resolves any conflicts. In most cases, you don't have to deal with hardware profiles.

- **Hot docking** If your notebook supports hot docking, you can safely plug the notebook into the docking station and remove it when the power is on. If your notebook does not support hot docking, you must turn the power off to your notebook and any devices connected to it before docking and undocking.

Don't Experiment! Check your notebook's documentation to determine whether it supports hot docking. If the notebook does not support hot docking and you dock it with the power on, you can severely damage the notebook and any devices connected to it.

Connecting Peripherals

As shown in Figure 10.1, the port replicator or docking station has ports that are similar to your notebook's built-in ports, enabling you to connect a mouse, keyboard, monitor, and other devices. Before you plug your notebook into the docking station or port replicator, connect the peripheral devices and plug in the docking station's AC adapter.

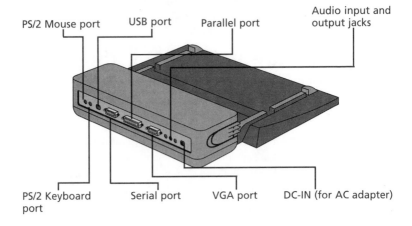

FIGURE 10.1 A port replicator contains ports that are nearly identical to those that are built into your notebook.

Docking and Undocking Your Notebook

The procedure for plugging a notebook into a docking station or port replicator varies greatly. You might need to completely turn off the power to all devices and to your notebook before docking it. Many notebooks require that a charged battery be loaded before docking or undocking, and some require that you press a special key combination. Follow the manufacturer's instructions.

Don't Take Chances   Carefully follow the manufacturer's instructions for docking and undocking your notebook. You can seriously damage your notebook by following the wrong procedure.

If your notebook PC supports Plug and Play *and* hot docking, you're in luck. To dock the PC, simply plug it into the docking station. To undock the PC, open the Start menu and click Eject PC. This tells Windows to revert to the undocked state and stop using the external devices. Release any clamps or clips on the docking station and slide the notebook out.

If your notebook does not support hot docking, or you're unsure, take the following steps to safely dock or undock your notebook:

1. If the notebook's power is already off, skip to step 5. If Windows is running, open the Windows Start menu and choose Shut Down.

2. Click Shut Down and click OK.

3. Wait until Windows shuts down the power to your notebook or displays a message indicating that it is safe to turn off your computer.

4. If the notebook power is still on, press and hold the power button for a couple seconds to turn it off.

5. Turn off any devices that are connected to the docking station or port replicator, such as a monitor or printer.

6. Take one of the following steps:

> *To dock the notebook:* Align the notebook's expansion port with the expansion socket on the docking station or port replicator and then slide the notebook gently into place until the port is firmly seated in the socket. If the docking station has clamps, secure them in place.

> *To undock the notebook:* Open the clamps or clips on the docking station to release the notebook and then gently slide the notebook out of the docking station.

Creating Hardware Profiles

Whenever you install a new device, you must install a hardware driver (software instructions that tell Windows how to use the device). As you add devices, Windows creates a hardware profile—a list of all installed devices—that Windows loads on startup.

 Plug and Play Notebook? If your notebook is Plug and Play compatible, skip these steps. Windows automatically determines which hardware to use when the notebook is docked or undocked. Windows even changes the display settings as needed to smoothly switch from the external monitor to the notebook display.

If your notebook does not have a plug-and-play BIOS (*Basic Input/Output System*) or if you do not have a docking station or port replicator, you must create two *hardware profiles* in Windows: one for the docked state and one for the undocked state. (If you connected devices to the notebook's built-in ports, consider it "docked.") To create a new hardware profile, take the following steps:

1. Alt+click My Computer.

2. Click the Hardware Profiles tab and click Original Configuration.

3. Click the Rename button so that you can call the Original Configuration "Undocked."

4. Type **Undocked** and click OK.

5. Click the Copy button to create a copy of the Undocked configuration and modify it to create a new "Docked" configuration.

6. Type **Docked** as the name of your new configuration and click OK (see Figure 10.2).

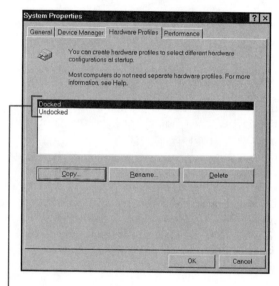

Hardware profiles

FIGURE 10.2   You should have two hardware profiles: Docked and Undocked.

7. Open the Start menu and click Shut Down.

8. Click Shut Down and click OK.

9. Plug your notebook into the docking station or connect the desired peripherals (mouse, keyboard, monitor) to the designated ports on the notebook.

10. Turn on the external devices, if necessary. In the case of a mouse or keyboard, no power is needed.

11. Turn on your notebook.

12. When Windows prompts you to choose a hardware profile, type the number for the Docked profile and press Enter.

13. Windows starts, detects the new devices, and installs the required drivers. If Windows fails to detect the new devices, open the Control Panel and click the Add New Hardware icon.

14. Follow the wizard's instructions to install drivers for the new devices.

 Working Backward Might Be Easier   If you already docked your notebook, ran Windows, and installed the devices, the Original Configuration contains a list of device drivers it will load whether your system is docked or not. In such a case, you'll need to work backward. Rename Original Configuration Docked, copy it to create a new configuration called Undocked, and then *disable* devices in the Undocked profile that are unavailable when the notebook is *not* connected to the docking station, as explained in the following section.

Disabling Devices in a Profile

Now that you have two hardware profiles, there might be some devices in a profile that you want to disable. For example, if, in the docked state, your notebook is connected to a mouse, you might want to disable the touchpad. Or, if there is a conflict between two similar devices (such as the notebook's monitor and a standard monitor), you must disable the device you don't want to use. Take the following steps to disable a device:

1. Alt+click My Computer.

2. Click the Hardware Profiles tab and click the profile that contains a device you want to disable.

3. Click the Device Manager tab.

4. Click the plus sign next to the type of device you want to disable.

5. Double-click the name of the device you want to disable.

6. Click Disable in this hardware profile and click OK (see Figure 10.3).

7. If needed, repeat step 6 to disable additional devices.

8. Click OK.

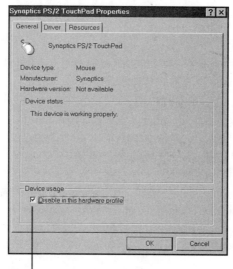

Click Disable in This Hardware Profile.

Figure 10.3   Disable any devices that are not connected to the PC in this hardware profile.

This lesson showed you how to make your notebook look and act more like a desktop PC by plugging it into a docking station or port replicator. The next lesson helps you prepare your notebook for a trip.

Traveling with Your Notebook: Pre-Flight Checklist

This lesson shows you how to prepare your notebook for a trip and use it in a car, an airplane, or a foreign country.

Planning a business trip is nerve-racking. You must book a flight and find a hotel or motel room that offers business accommodations. You pack your bags and pat your pockets making sure you have your plane ticket, itinerary, charge cards, and cash. And you try to find a loyal friend to get you to the airport...on time.

A notebook further complicates matters. You must charge the batteries; make sure you have all the programs and files you need; and pack any PC cards, cables, and adapters you need for making connections on the road. This lesson acts as your laptop valet, making sure you haven't forgotten anything.

Finding Notebook-Friendly Accommodations

You can count on any hotel or motel to supply a few power outlets and a phone line, but if you need any additional equipment, such as a printer or fax machine, you might be out of luck. When making your reservations, ask about accommodations for business travelers. Make sure the room has a three-prong, grounded outlet and a separate phone line for your modem.

Some rooms come with a fax machine and a printer or enable you to rent the equipment you need. Other establishments might have a business center.

Even if the room does offer the basic amenities for a business traveler, you should bring along some basic equipment:

- **Three-prong adapter** If the room has outlets for two-pronged plugs, you'll need an adapter to plug in your notebook. Also bring a small, flat-head screwdriver so that you can ground the adapter using the outlet's cover plate screw.

- **Portable surge suppressor** Most computer stores carry portable surge suppressors that include two power outlets and two or three phone jacks. This is a useful accessory even if you use the notebook in your home or office (see Figure 11.1).

FIGURE 11.1 A direct, plug-in surge suppressor with phone jacks is a useful addition to your notebook. (Photo courtesy of Tripp Lite, Chicago, IL.)

- **Extension cord** You can usually move the desk or table in a motel room to place it near the desired power outlet, but an extension cord gives you greater flexibility.

- **One-to-two phone jack adapter** If the room has only one phone jack, use the adapter to connect both the phone and your modem. If your notebook's modem has two phone jacks or you have a surge suppressor with two or more phone jacks, you can do without this adapter.

- **Phone line tester**   Many hotels and businesses are equipped with digital phone lines that can damage your modem. A phone line tester has an indicator light that shows whether the line is a digital (dangerous) line or analog (safe) line.

- **Windows CD**   The Windows CD has drivers for thousands of devices. If you need to borrow a device, such as a printer or modem, you can install the required driver from the Windows CD.

- **Fax modem**   Make sure you have a fax modem for your note-book and that the fax software is installed. Many hotels and motels charge a steep fee for using their fax machine.

Before You Leave: Savvy Planning and Preparation

Toting along a notebook on a business trip is like traveling with a child. The notebook has its own carry-on baggage, and you must make sure it is properly packed and ready to go. Use the following checklist to make sure:

- **Remove any CDs from the CD-ROM drive**   You don't want a loose CD rattling around inside your notebook.

- **Enable the power-saving features**   If you disabled the power-saving features, enable them so that they will be on when you start using the notebook.

- **Test any hardware or software you plan on using**   One of the biggest mistakes people make is to take a new hardware device on the road and forget the installation disk that's required for installing the device. Make sure everything is working properly before you head out.

- **Take any data files you might need**   If you need documents that are stored on your desktop PC, see Lesson 12, "Taking

Work on the Road with Windows Briefcase," to learn how to safely transfer the document files to your notebook.

- **Fully charge the battery**   If you're flying on a plane, load the battery into the notebook so that you can turn on the notebook when airport security asks you to and you can use your notebook in-flight if the plane doesn't have a power source for notebooks. If you have another battery, charge it, too.

- **Remove any PC cards**   PC cards can consume battery power even when inactive. Remove the cards, place them in their protective cases, and pack them in your notebook carrying case.

- **Pack your AC adapter**   If you run low on battery power, you'll need to plug in your notebook and recharge the battery.

- **Pack a phone cord for your modem**   Most computer and electronics stores carry retractable extension cords for modems. The cord rolls into a case and you pull out only the length you need (see Figure 11.2).

FIGURE 11.2   A retractable phone cord lets you use only the length of cord you need. (Photo courtesy of Port, Incorporated.)

- **Pack any external devices you might need**   If you have an external floppy or CD-ROM drive, stick it in the carrying case.

This is especially important if you use programs that access the CD.

- **Set up your desktop PC for remote access**   If you forget a file, you can connect to your desktop PC via modem and copy the file. See Lesson 14, "Remote Computing Via Modem," for instructions.

Surviving Airport Security

Airport security doesn't like to see people carrying any electronic devices on airplanes, especially notebooks. The security person will ask you to open the notebook and turn on the power to make sure it is operating. He or she will then place the notebook on a table beyond the gates while you pass through security, which provides an ideal opportunity for someone to walk off with your notebook.

The following tips will help you and your notebook breeze through the security gates and prevent someone from taking your notebook:

- **Load a charged battery**   The security person will ask you to turn on your notebook. You don't want to have to plug it in or load a battery at the gate.

- **Write down the notebook's serial number**   If your notebook is lost or stolen, this number will help you identify it and fill out a police report.

- **Mark your notebook's carrying case**   There are dozens of black notebook carrying cases in airports. Use a bright-colored strap or place a couple of stickers on the case so that you can easily see if someone is walking off with your notebook. Better yet, use a bag that doesn't look like a notebook carrying case.

- **Give yourself extra time**   Give yourself sufficient time to check your bags and pass through security. Delays and thefts usually occur when you're too hurried to be careful.

- **Place any metal objects you're carrying in a tray**   The faster you get through security, the less time you will be separated from your notebook.

- **Place your bags on the conveyor belt first**   By checking your bags through first, you can concentrate on your notebook.

- **Keep an eye on it**   When the security person takes your notebook, keep an eye on the notebook and ask the security person to watch your notebook until you pick it up. If you're traveling with someone else, ask that person to go through first and keep an eye on the notebook.

Watch Out for This Trick   One of the standard tricks of the trade requires two thieves. Both people stand in front of you at the security gate. One goes through the gate and waits for your notebook at the end of the conveyor belt while the other sets off the metal detector to tie you up.

More Anti-Theft Strategies and Tips   See Lesson 23, "Securing Your Notebook: Anti-Theft Guide," for additional tips and information about security products.

Using Your Notebook in Flight

Airplanes don't feature the ideal environment for computing, but if you can balance your notebook on a flight tray, you might be able to fit in a couple hours of productive work or while away the time with your favorite computer games.

To use the notebook safely, remember to turn off its power on take-offs and landings as requested by the airline. There is no hard proof that electronic devices interfere with the navigational instruments on airplanes, but don't take chances. To protect your notebook during take-off and landing, store it under the seat in front of you, not in an overhead compartment.

To power your notebook in flight, you have the following two options:

- If you have a fully charged battery or two, you can run the notebook off the battery.

- Some airplanes, typically those used for long flights, are equipped with power outlets (in the First Class or Business sections) designed specifically for notebooks. They're similar to cigarette-lighter sockets in cars. You can plug your notebook into the power outlet by using an emPower adapter (see Figure 11.3).

FIGURE 11.3   An emPower adapter lets you plug your notebook into special power outlets available on some flights. (Photo courtesy of Port, Incorporated.)

 Make Sure It's Designed for Your Notebook   Use only an emPower adapter that's specifically designed for your notebook. The adapter converts the source power into a specific voltage. If you use the wrong adapter for your notebook, you could damage it.

See Appendix B   For a list of manufacturers and suppliers of notebook batteries, power adapters, and other useful accessories, check out Appendix B, "Notebook Suppliers."

DVD for All the Comforts of Home   To make the most of your flight, consider purchasing a DVD player, a few DVD movies, and a pair of headphones. If you don't like the movie on the airline, play your own. If you have a CD player, bring along a few of your favorite audio CDs. Keep in mind that CD-ROM and DVD drives are power hogs.

Using (and Charging) Your Notebook in Your Car

Although you probably do little typing when you're behind the wheel, you might want to work when a business associate is driving or charge your notebook when you're driving from one company to another. When you're in your car, you can charge the battery using your car's cigarette lighter socket and an emPower adapter, as explained in the previous section.

When transporting or storing your notebook in your car, take the following precautions:

- **Avoid excessive heat**   Don't leave your notebook in the car or trunk during hot summer days. In addition, try to keep the notebook out of direct sunlight.

- **Avoid excessive cold**   Extremely cold temperatures can make the plastic case and other components more brittle. Handle the notebook gently when moving it. Also, before using a cold notebook, let it warm to room temperature for a couple of hours. A sudden change in temperature can cause moisture to form inside the case; you need to allow this moisture to dissipate.

- **Keep heavy objects off the case**   Although this is always a precaution, a car ride exposes the case to additional vibrations, making the notebook case and hard drive more susceptible to damage. Likewise, don't let the notebook slide around loose in the trunk.

Built Tough   Some notebooks are specially designed for rough handling. For example, Panasonic's ToughBook is designed with a magnesium alloy case, water-resistant keyboard, and shock-mounted hard drive. Another tough notebook is the Dell Latitude, which has passed the notebook torture test for five years running.

Traveling to Foreign Lands

When traveling abroad, be prepared. Your destination might not have the same power supplies and phone lines you're accustomed to using at home. Contact your notebook manufacturer or visit its Web site to determine whether any travel kits are available for the country you'll be visiting (see Figure 11.4) or assemble your own kit using the following list as your guide:

- **Voltage adapter**   When traveling abroad, find out the type of voltage adapter you'll need and obtain one before you hit the road. Your notebook's AC adapter might have a switch you can flip to change the voltage input, in which case you might be able to do without a voltage adapter. However, you'll still need an adapter plug for the outlet.

Choose the Right Voltage   If your AC adapter has a switch for changing the voltage input, make sure you flip the switch back when you return home. Choosing the wrong voltage setting can destroy your notebook.

- **Phone line adapter**   If you are traveling abroad, don't assume that the phone jacks match the ones you use at home. Obtain the required adapter and bring it along. You should also have a phone line tester, as explained earlier.

- **Phone line noise filter**   You might encounter phone connections that are not modem-friendly. In some European countries, the phone lines carry noise, called *tax*, which is used to monitor usage. This noise can foul up your Internet and fax communications. A noise filter helps reduce the effect.

- **Proof of ownership**   When traveling abroad, check customs laws and carry proof of ownership of your notebook. You don't want customs inspectors to seize your notebook.

- **Dialing codes for calling home**   Foreign countries might require a special dialing code to reach numbers in your home country. In addition, you might not be able to use toll-free numbers when you're on the road, so obtain toll numbers for companies and online services you might need to call. (See Lesson 15, "Accessing Your Internet Connection on the Road," for details.)

FIGURE 11.4   A travel kit typically contains all the tools and adapters your notebook needs. (Photo courtesy of Port, Incorporated.)

Phone Line Tester/Noise Filter/Surge Suppressor
A combination unit can test the phone line to determine whether it is an analog or digital line, filter out any noise, and protect your notebook from power surges carried through the phone line.

This lesson showed you how to prepare your notebook for road trips and use it efficiently when traveling to foreign lands. The next lesson shows you how to safely transfer files between your notebook and desktop PCs.

LESSON 12

Taking Work on the Road with Windows Briefcase

This lesson shows you how to transfer documents between your notebook and desktop PC without accidentally replacing the new version of a document with the old version.

If you have both a notebook and desktop PC, you probably need to transfer files from your desktop PC to your notebook to take work with you on trips. If you edit the files on your notebook, you must then copy them back to the desktop PC to ensure that you have the most recent versions on both PCs.

Of course, you can exchange files between your notebook and desktop PC by using My Computer or Windows Explorer to transfer the files with a floppy disk. However, this is not the most efficient or secure method. If you happen to forget which files are the most recent, you run the risk of replacing the new versions with older ones. This lesson shows you how to prevent accidental replacements.

Understanding Briefcase

Windows offers a convenient tool for safely transferring files between PCs: Briefcase. With Briefcase, you open an electronic "briefcase," copy the desired files to it, and then drag the Briefcase icon to your floppy disk icon. Windows copies all the files in the Briefcase to the floppy disk. Briefcase also keeps track of file versions to help prevent you from accidentally overwriting newer files with their older versions. When you copy files back to your desktop PC, Briefcase indicates which files are more recent.

Installing Briefcase

If there is no My Briefcase icon on your Windows desktop, it might not be installed. Take the following steps to install Briefcase on both your notebook and desktop PC:

1. Click the Start button, point to Settings, and click Control Panel.

2. Click Add/Remove Programs.

3. In the Add/Remove Programs Properties dialog box, click the Windows Setup tab.

4. In the Components list, double-click Accessories.

5. Click the check box next to Briefcase to place a check in the box (see Figure 12.1).

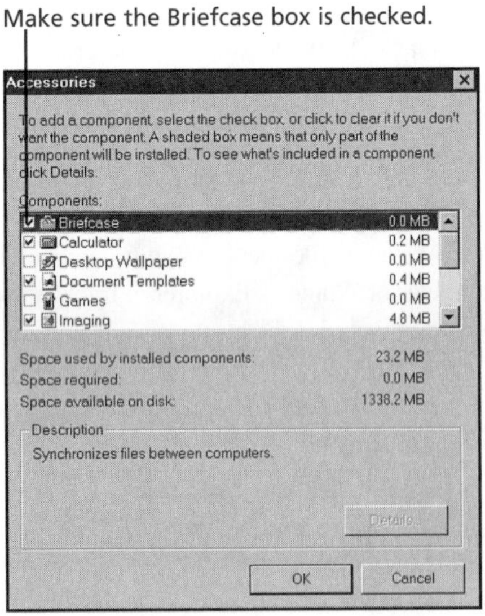

Make sure the Briefcase box is checked.

FIGURE 12.1   Install Briefcase on both your notebook and desktop PC.

6. Click OK to return to the Add/Remove Programs Properties dialog box.

7. Click OK to save the setting.

8. If prompted to insert the Windows CD, insert the CD in your CD-ROM drive and click OK.

9. Repeat the steps, if needed, to install Briefcase on your other PC.

You should now have a Briefcase icon on the Windows desktop on both your notebook and desktop PC. To quickly add a new Briefcase at any time, right-click the desktop and choose New, Briefcase.

Taking Files on the Road

Before you leave on a trip, you should pack any document files you might need in Briefcase and then transfer Briefcase to a floppy disk. Take the following steps:

1. In Windows Explorer or My Computer, select the folder or file you want to place in your Briefcase.

2. Right-click one of the selected items, point to Send To, and click My Briefcase (see Figure 12.2).

3. If the Welcome to the Windows Briefcase dialog box appears, click Finish to copy the selected items to your Briefcase.

4. Insert a blank disk into the floppy disk drive and then drag and drop the My Briefcase icon over the floppy disk icon. (Or, right-click My Briefcase, point to Send To, and click 3fi Floppy.)

5. Remove the floppy disk.

6. Insert the floppy disk into your notebook's floppy drive.

7. Run My Computer and click the floppy drive icon.

8. Drag and drop the My Briefcase icon onto the Windows desktop.

Right-click a file.

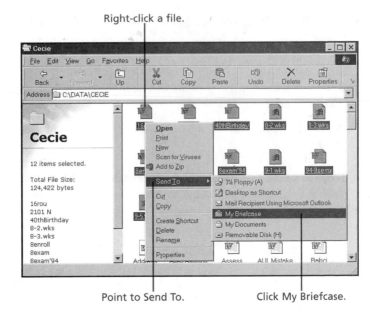

Point to Send To.   Click My Briefcase.

FIGURE 12.2   Transfer folder and file to My Briefcase.

 Transfer Briefcase Over a Direct Cable Connection   If your notebook does not have a floppy drive, connect the two computers using a data cable, as explained in Lesson 13, "Connecting Your Notebook and Desktop PCs." You can then copy My Briefcase from your desktop PC to your notebook.

Opening Files from Briefcase

When you're on the road, you can open document files directly from Briefcase, just as if it were a folder on your hard drive. Take the following steps to open a document from Briefcase:

1. Run the program you want to use to open the file and choose its File, Open command.

2. Open the Look In drop-down list and click My Briefcase. The
   Open dialog box displays the contents of the Briefcase (see
   Figure 12.3).

3. Click the name of the document you want to open and click the
   Open button.

Click My Briefcase.   Click the Open button.

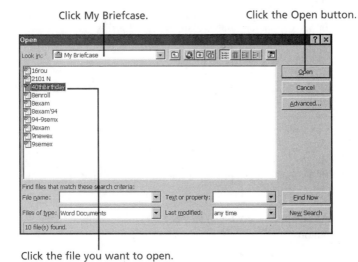

Click the file you want to open.

FIGURE 12.3 Open files from Briefcase and save them to Briefcase
as if Briefcase were a folder.

Returning Files to Your Desktop PC

When you return from your trip, take the following steps to copy your
document files from your notebook back to your desktop PC:

1. Insert a disk into your notebook's floppy drive.

2. Double-click My Computer and resize the window so that you
   can see both the My Briefcase icon and the icon for your floppy
   disk drive on the desktop.

3. Drag and drop the My Briefcase icon onto the icon for your
   floppy disk.

4. Eject the floppy disk.

5. Insert the disk into your desktop PC's floppy drive and click the floppy drive's icon in My Computer.

6. Double-click My Computer on the desktop PC and resize the My Computer window so that you can see a blank area of the Windows desktop.

7. In My Computer, double-click the icon for drive A. My Computer displays the contents of the disk in drive A, which should consist of My Briefcase.

8. Drag and drop the My Briefcase icon onto the Windows desktop.

9. Click the My Briefcase icon to display its contents.

10. Click the Update All button.

11. If desired, you can prevent a file from being updated by right-clicking it and choosing Skip (see Figure 12.4).

12. After marking any files you want to skip, click the Update button.

To skip a file, right-click it and click Skip.

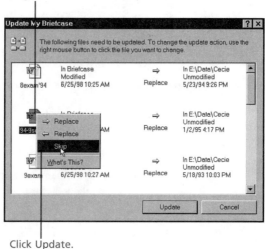

Click Update.

FIGURE **12.4**   Briefcase shows you which files are newer versions.

This lesson showed you how to transfer files safely between your notebook and desktop PC. The next lesson shows you how to connect your notebook and desktop PCs with a cable for faster file transfers without using a floppy disk.

LESSON 13

Connecting Your Notebook and Desktop PCs

This lesson shows you how to connect your notebook and desktop PCs with a cable to create your own mini-network.

Windows includes a feature called Direct Cable Connection that enables you to connect two computers by using a serial or parallel *data* cable. When the computers are connected, you can use one computer to link to the other computer and use its files, programs, and printer just as if you were working on a network.

Direct Cable Connection is especially useful for transferring large amounts of data from one computer to another. You simply copy a folder from one computer, switch to the other computer, and paste the folder on the desired hard disk. This lesson shows you how to establish the necessary connections and share files and other resources.

Connecting the Data Cable

To connect your notebook and desktop PC, you must obtain a data cable for the serial or parallel ports or use a USB cable. When shopping for and installing the data cable, keep the following points in mind:

- The cable must be a *data transfer* cable. You cannot use a standard serial modem cable or parallel printer cable. (You can, however, purchase a null-modem adapter to convert a serial modem cable into a data transfer cable.)

- Some data cables come with both serial and parallel port connectors. However, do not connect the serial port on one PC to the parallel port on the other; you want a parallel-to-parallel or serial-to-serial port connection.

- Some desktop PCs have two serial ports: 9-pin and 25-pin. You can plug a 9-pin connector into a 25-pin outlet by using a special 9-to-25 pin adapter.

After you obtain the proper cable, take the following steps to connect the two PCs:

1. Shut down Windows on both your notebook and the desktop PCs.

2. Turn off your notebook and the desktop PCs.

3. Connect the data cable to the serial or parallel ports on both PCs, as shown in Figure 13.1.

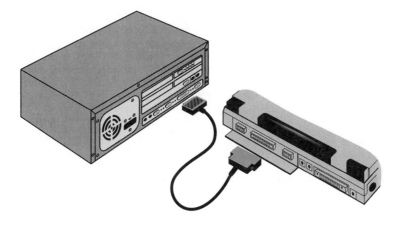

FIGURE 13.1 With both PCs off, connect the cable to the serial or parallel port on each PC.

Installing the Windows Networking Components

In order to establish a direct cable connection, you must install the following Windows networking components on your notebook and desktop PC:

- **Dial-Up Networking** is essential for establishing any network or direct cable connection.

- **Direct Cable Connection** is a Windows utility that enables two PCs to transfer data over a data cable.

To install the required Windows networking components, take the following steps:

1. In the Windows Control Panel, click the Add/Remove Programs icon.

2. Click the Windows Setup tab to display a list of component categories.

3. In the Components list, click Communications.

4. Click the Details button.

5. Click the boxes next to Dial-Up Networking and Direct Cable Connection to place a check in each box (see Figure 13.2).

6. Click OK to return to the Add/Remove Programs Properties dialog box.

7. Click OK to save your changes.

8. If prompted to insert the Windows CD, insert the CD into your CD-ROM drive and click OK.

9. If prompted to restart your computer, save any open documents, close all running programs, and click Yes.

10. If necessary, repeat the steps on your other PC to install the Windows networking components.

Place a check mark next to Dial-Up Networking.

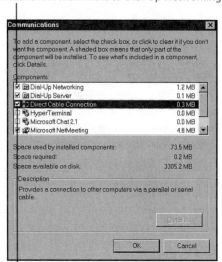

Place a check mark next to Direct Cable Connection.

FIGURE 13.2 Install Dial-Up Networking and Direct Cable Connection.

Adding Network Protocols and Services

After the network components are installed, you must install network protocols and services. The following list explains the three most popular network protocols:

- **TCP/IP** is primarily for Internet access.

- **NetBEUI** is used for fast data transfers over a network or direct cable connection.

- **IPX/SPX** is used for playing multi-player games over a network connection and functions as a network protocol for Netware networks.

Protocol A *protocol* is a set of rules that govern the exchange of data over the connection. Think of a protocol as a language that your two PCs agree to speak.

Network *services* enable PCs to share resources on the network. You should install two services: Client for Microsoft Networks (which provides general network support) and File and Printer Sharing (which enables your two PCs to share data files and printers).

To install the required protocol (NetBEUI) and services, take the following steps:

1. In the Control Panel, click the Network icon. The Network dialog box appears, displaying a list of installed protocols.

2. Click the Add button. The Select Network Component Type dialog box appears.

3. Click Client and then click Add.

4. Click Microsoft, click Client for Microsoft Networks, and then click OK.

5. Click the Add button.

6. Click Protocol and click the Add button. The Select Network Protocol dialog box lists manufacturers and network protocols.

7. In the Manufacturers list, click Microsoft.

8. Click NetBEUI to add the protocol required for your direct cable connection.

9. Click OK. You are returned to the Network dialog box, where the new protocol is added to the list of network components (see Figure 13.3).

Make sure Client for
Microsoft Networks is listed.

Choose Client for Microsoft
Networks as your primary logon.

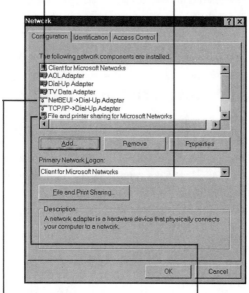

NetBEUI is the required protocol
for your cable connection.

File and Printer Sharing must be on.

FIGURE 13.3 You must install the required protocol and services.

10. Open the Primary Network Logon drop-down list and choose
Client for Microsoft Networks.

11. Click the File and Print Sharing button.

12. Select the desired sharing option to share file, printer, or both
and click OK. You are returned to the Network dialog box.

13. Click the Identification tab and enter a name for this PC in the
Computer Name text box, for example, Central or Notebook.
This name gives the PC a unique identity.

14. Click in the Workgroup text box and type the name for your
workgroup. Use the same workgroup name for both PCs.

15. Click the Access Control tab and make sure Share-Level Access Control is selected. This enables you to assign different access privileges to each PC.

16. Click OK.

Activating Your Direct Cable Connection

Direct Cable Connection leads you through the required steps to set up one PC as the *host* and the other as the *guest*. The host is usually the more powerful of the two PCs. If you are connecting a desktop and notebook PC, the desktop PC will typically be the host. Take the following steps to activate the connection:

1. On the desktop PC, click the Start button, point to Programs, Accessories, Communications, and click Direct Cable Connection. The Direct Cable Connection Wizard appears.

2. Click Host and then click Next (see Figure 13.4). You are prompted to pick the port in which you plugged the cable.

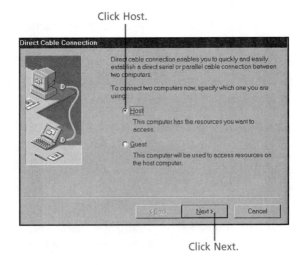

Click Host.

Click Next.

Figure 13.4   Set up the desktop PC as the host.

3. Select the port to which you connected the data transfer cable and click Next.

4. On your notebook, click the Start button, point to Programs, Accessories, Communications, and click Direct Cable Connection.

5. Click Guest and click Next. You are prompted to pick the port in which you plugged the cable.

6. Select the port and click Next.

7. Go back to the desktop PC and click Finish. The desktop PC displays a dialog box indicating that it is waiting for the guest (notebook) PC to connect.

8. On the notebook PC, click Finish.

Sharing Disks, Folders, Files, and Printers

In order for one PC (the guest) to access disks, folders, files, and printers on another PC (the host), the host must give the guest permission to share the resource. You can share resources in either of the following modes:

- **Full access** enables the guest PC to use files on the host just as if those files were stored on its own hard drive. The guest PC can open a file, modify it, and save it to the host's hard disk and copy, move, and delete files on the host PC.

- **Read-only access** permits the guest PC to open files and copy files from the host PC's hard disk. It does not enable the guest PC to save a modified file to the host, delete files from the host's hard disk, or copy files to the host's hard disk.

 Sharing Works Both Ways   Just as the guest PC can access the host's files, the host can access the guest's files, assuming you mark resources on the guest as shared.

To mark a disk drive, folder, or printer as a shared resource, take the
following steps:

1. Right-click the icon for the disk, folder, or printer you want to
   share and click Sharing. The Properties dialog box for the
   selected resource appears with the Sharing tab in front (see
   Figure 13.5).

2. Click Shared As. The Share Name text box automatically displays the drive letter or the folder or printer name.

Turn on Shared As.   Name the resource.   Enter a description, if desired.

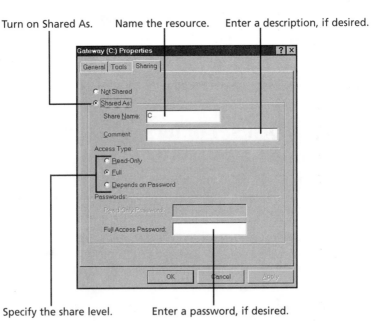

Specify the share level.   Enter a password, if desired.

FIGURE 13.5 Before the guest can share a resource on the host,
you must mark the resource as shared on the host PC.

3. If desired, type a different name for the drive, folder, or printer.

4. (Optional) Type a brief description of the resource in the
   Comment text box.

5. Under Access Type, choose the desired share option: Read-Only or Full.

Password Required? If you were setting up your PC for network use, you could use the Password option to require another user on the network to enter a password for full access. Because you're setting up a direct cable connection between two computers you use, you can ignore this option.

6. Click OK. You are returned to My Computer or Windows Explorer and a hand appears below the icon for the shared disk, folder, or printer.

To terminate sharing, right-click the icon for the disk, folder, or printer and choose Sharing. Select Not Shared and click OK.

Use Your Desktop's Floppy Drive If you find it inconvenient to connect and disconnect your notebook's floppy drive, mark your desktop's floppy drive as shared. You can even share CD-ROM and DVD drives!

Accessing Resources with Network Neighborhood

To use one PC (the host or guest) to access disks, folders, and files on the other PC, use the Network Neighborhood. When you click the Network Neighborhood icon on the Windows desktop, Network Neighborhood displays an icon for the other PC. You can then browse the shared resources, just as if they were on your PC. To share resources, take the following steps:

1. On the Windows desktop, click the Network Neighborhood icon.

2. Click the icon for the other PC. A folder is displayed for each shared drive and folder on the other PC (see Figure 13.6). Note that drive icons appear as folders.

Click or double-click an icon to view the contents of the disk or folder.

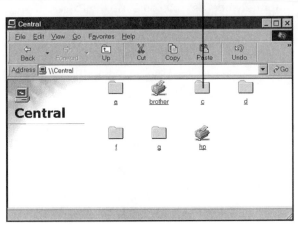

FIGURE 13.6 Network Neighborhood displays icons for the shared disks and folders.

3. Click the icon for the disk or folder you want to access. Folders and files appear as if they were on this PC's hard disk.

4. If you have full access to the disk and folder, you can copy files from one PC to the other simply by dragging and dropping or using the Copy and Paste commands.

5. If you try to enter a command that you do not have permission to enter on the other PC, an error message appears indicating that the PC has denied you access. Click OK.

Additional Access You can also access the Network Neighborhood by selecting it from the Address drop-down list in My Computer, from the folder list in Windows Explorer, from the Look in drop-down list in the Open dialog box (File, Open), and from the Save in drop-down list in the Save dialog box (File, Save As).

Mapping a Drive or Folder to Your Computer

If you frequently access a particular disk or folder on one PC, you can *map* the disk or folder to a drive on the other PC. For example, if your notebook has a hard drive C and a CD-ROM drive D, you can map drive C on the desktop PC as drive E on your notebook. The drive will then appear in the following windows and dialog boxes:

- **My Computer** The drive appears in the opening My Computer window as a network drive.

- **Windows Explorer** The drive appears in the folder list (left pane) in Windows Explorer.

- **File lists** If you choose File, Save or File, Open in your applications, you can open the Look in or Save in drop-down list and choose the mapped drive, just as if it were installed on your PC.

To map a folder or drive on one PC to a drive on your other PC, take the following steps:

1. In the Network Neighborhood, right-click the drive or folder on the other PC that you want to map to this PC and click Map Network Drive. The Map Network Drive dialog box appears, as shown in Figure 13.7.

Select a drive letter.   Click OK.

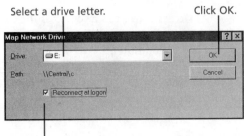

To reconnect to the drive on startup, turn on Reconnect at Logon.

Figure 13.7   To map a drive, assign it a drive letter that your PC does not use for a local drive (or a network drive when your notebook is docked).

2. Open the Drive drop-down list and choose a drive letter to assign to the network disk or folder.

3. To have Windows automatically identify this disk or folder on startup, click Reconnect at Logon.

4. Click OK.

Sharing a Printer

You probably don't have separate printers for your desktop and notebook PCs. However, you can share a printer over the direct cable connection. In order to share the printer, you must install the printer on your notebook. Take the following steps:

1. Click the Start button, point to Settings, and click Printers. The contents of the Printers folder appears.

2. Click the Add Printer icon. The Add Printer Wizard appears.

3. Click Next. The Wizard asks if you want to install a local or network printer.

4. Click Network Printer and click Next. The Wizard prompts you to specify the path to the printer.

5. Click the Browse button. The Browse for Printer dialog box displays icons for the desktop PC and notebook.

6. If necessary, click the plus sign next to the icon for your desktop PC. The printer's icon appears, as shown in Figure 13.8.

Click the icon for the printer you want to install.

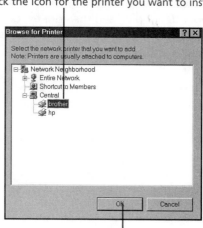

Click OK.

FIGURE 13.8   You can install a network printer to use as if it were connected to your notebook.

7. Click the printer's icon and click OK. You are returned to the Wizard, which displays the path to the printer.

8. Click Next. The Wizard displays the name of the printer as it appears on the desktop PC. You can change the name, if desired.

9. To use this printer as the default printer for all of your Windows applications, click Yes. Click Next. The Wizard now asks if you want to print a test page.

10. Click Yes or No and click Finish. If you chose to print a test page, the Wizard sends the page to the printer. Windows copies the necessary printer files from the desktop PC to your notebook and returns you to the Printers folder. An icon for the printer appears.

Defer Printing on the Road   When you're on the road, you might want to defer printing to a later time. Right-click your printer icon and click Use Printer Offline. Print your documents as you normally would. When you're ready to print, connect the printer to your notebook or establish a Direct Cable Connection with your desktop PC and then right-click the printer icon and choose Use Printer Offline to start printing.

This lesson showed you how to use the Windows Direct Cable Connection utility to connect your notebook and desktop PCs and share files and other resources. In the next lesson, you learn how to connect to your desktop PC via modem when you're out of town.

Lesson 14

Remote Computing Via Modem

This lesson shows you how to connect to your desktop PC or network when you're on the road.

You thought you transferred to your notebook all the document files you needed for your trip, but when you arrive, you realize that you forgot an important file. Are you completely out of luck? Maybe not. If your desktop PC is set up to answer the phone, you can dial into it using your notebook's modem and download the file. In addition, if your desktop PC is networked, you can access the network's files and resources. This lesson shows you just what to do.

Installing the Dial-Up Server Utility

In order to have your desktop PC answer the phone, you must install the Windows networking components and the Dial-Up Server utility. To install the required components, take the following steps on your desktop PC:

1. In the Windows Control Panel, click the Add/Remove Programs icon.

2. Click the Windows Setup tab to display a list of component categories.

3. In the Components list, click Communications.

4. Click the Details button.

5. Make sure the Dial-Up Networking box is checked and click the box next to Dial-Up Server to place a check in the box (see Figure 14.1).

Choose Dial-Up Networking.

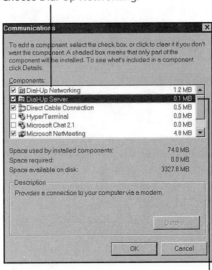

Choose Dial-Up Server.

FIGURE 14.1   Install Dial-Up Networking and Dial-Up Server.

6. Click OK to return to the Add/Remove Programs Properties dialog box.

7. Click OK to save your changes.

8. If prompted to insert the Windows CD, insert the CD into your CD-ROM drive and click OK.

9. If prompted to restart your computer, save any open documents, close all running programs, and click Yes.

You must also install Dial-Up Networking on your notebook and install the following on both your notebook and desktop PC:

- Dial-Up Adapter enables the computers to establish a modem connection.

- TCP/IP (Transmission Control Protocol/Internet Protocol) enables two computers to transfer data via modem.

- Client for Microsoft Networks is a service that enables you to log on to a PC using another PC over a modem, network, or direct cable connection.

- File and Printer Sharing enables you to mark disks, folders, and printers as shared resources.

Refer to Lesson 13, "Connecting Your Notebook and Desktop PCs," to learn how to install network protocols and services. However, instead of installing the NetBEUI protocol, install TCP/IP, if it is not already installed (see Figure 14.2).

Client for Microsoft Networks   Dial-Up Adapter

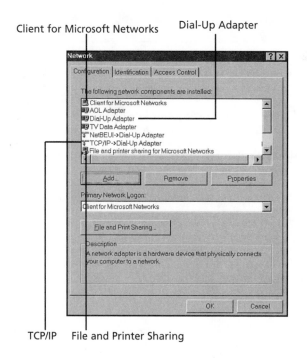

TCP/IP   File and Printer Sharing

FIGURE 14.2   Make sure your notebook and desktop PC have the required network services and protocols installed.

Designating Shared Resources

Unless you flag a disk or folder as shared, you won't be able to access it from a remote location. Your desktop PC will answer the phone and establish the connection, but will not give you access to disks, folders, or files.

Everything on a Shared Disk Is Shared   If you mark a disk as shared, all files and folders on that disk are shared. To share an individual folder or file, mark the disk as Unshared and then mark the individual files or folders as shared.

To mark a disk or folder as a shared resource, take the following steps:

1. Right-click the icon for the disk or folder you want to share and click Sharing. The Properties dialog box for the selected resource appears with the Sharing tab in front (see Figure 14.3).

2. Click Shared As. The Share Name text box automatically displays the drive letter or folder or printer name.

3. If desired, type a different name for the drive or folder.

4. (Optional) Type a brief description of the resource in the Comment text box.

5. Under Access Type, choose the desired share option: Read-Only or Full.

Turn on Shared As.   Name the resource.   Enter a description, if desired.

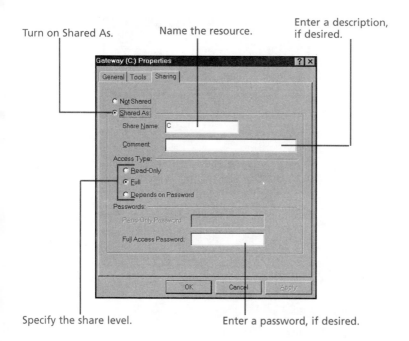

Specify the share level.   Enter a password, if desired.

FIGURE 14.3 To enable your notebook to copy a file from the desktop or network, mark the disk or folder as shared.

Setting Up Your Desktop PC to Answer the Phone

After you install Dial-Up Server, you can enter settings to instruct it to answer the phone and prompt you for a password. The password feature is important because it prevents an unauthorized user from dialing into your desktop PC and deleting files or causing other damage.

To enter settings for Dial-Up Server, take the following steps:

1. On your desktop PC, open My Computer and click the Dial-Up Networking icon.

2. Open the Connections menu and click Dial-Up Server. The Dial-Up Server dialog box appears, as shown in Figure 14.4.

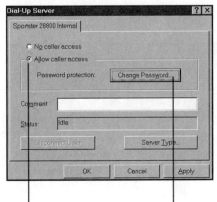

Turn on Allow Caller Access.   Assign an access password.

FIGURE 14.4   Use the Dial-Up Server dialog box to enable your PC to answer the phone.

3. Click Allow Caller Access.

4. Click the Change Password button.

5. Click in the New password text box and type the desired password.

Choose Your Password Carefully   Choose a password that is easy for you to remember but tough for someone else to guess. If you forget your password, you won't be able to access your desktop PC via modem.

6. Click in the Confirm new password text box, type the password again, and click OK.

7. Click OK. A Dial-Up Server icon appears in the system tray, indicating that your desktop PC is now ready to answer the phone.

Before you leave on your big trip, make sure you turn on your desktop
PC, or it won't answer the phone.

 Disable Any Automatic Internet Connections   If your
desktop PC is set up to automatically connect to the
Internet to download subscribed Web content or
email messages, consider disabling these features or
entering preferences to tell your Internet programs to
hang up after performing the tasks. If your desktop
PC is connected to the Internet when you try to call it,
you'll get a busy signal.

Creating a New Dial-Up Connection on Your Notebook

In order to dial into your desktop PC using your notebook, you must create a new Dial-Up Connection icon on your notebook. Clicking the icon
tells Windows to dial up your desktop PC and establish a connection. To
create a new Dial-Up Connection icon, take the following steps:

1. On your notebook computer, double-click My Computer.

2. Double-click the Dial-Up Networking icon.

3. Double-click the Make New Connection icon.

4. Type a name for the connection, such as **Desktop**, select your
   modem, and click Next.

5. Type the area code and telephone number for the phone line to
   which your desktop PC's modem is connected and choose the
   country in which your desktop PC resides, as shown in Figure
   14.5. Click Next.

6. Click Finish.

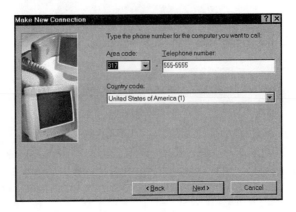

FIGURE 14.5 Type the area code and phone number for your desktop PC.

Changing Your Modem's Dialing Properties

When you're on the road, you must provide instructions that tell Windows where you are so that Windows can determine how to dial from your current location. You provide these instructions in the Dialing Properties dialog box. Take the following steps:

1. In the Windows Control Panel, double-click the Telephony icon. The Dialing Properties dialog box appears, as shown in Figure 14.6.

2. Click the New button. A dialog box appears indicating that a new location has been created.

3. Click OK.

4. Type a name for the remote location in the I am dialing from text box.

5. Open the I am in this country/region drop-down list and choose the geographical area of your remote location.

Enter any special numbers you need to dial.

Choose the country.

Type a name for your location.

Choose the area code for your remote location.

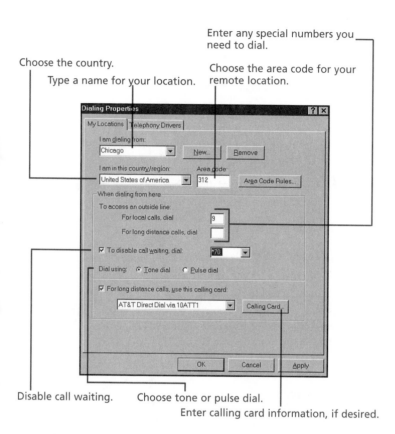

Disable call waiting.   Choose tone or pulse dial.

Enter calling card information, if desired.

FIGURE 14.6 In order for Windows to dial properly, it needs to know where you are.

6. Click in the Area Code text box and type the area code for the selected geographical location. This tells your modem to dial an area code only when the area code differs from the area code of your current location.

7. In the When Dialing from Here section, enter any numbers you must dial to access an outside line. For example, you might have to dial 9 to dial out from a motel room. Do not type "1" in the For Long Distance Calls, Dial text box. Type a number only if you need to dial a special code before dialing the generic 1 commonly required for placing long-distance calls.

8. If you have call waiting, click to place a check mark next to To Disable Call Waiting, Dial ___ and then enter the number required to disable call waiting in your area. (This is usually *70, but check the phone book.)

9. If you plan to use a calling card to place long distance calls, click to place a check mark next to For Long Distance Calls, Use This Calling Card and then click the Calling Card button.

10. In the Change Calling Card dialog box, enter the requested calling card information and click OK.

11. Click OK to save your settings.

After you enter the Telephony settings for the remote location, Windows assumes the notebook is at that location. When you return from your trip (or if you plan on using the notebook before you leave), you must change the settings back. Click the Telephony icon and then open the I am dialing from drop-down list and choose New Location. (Windows saves the default dialing properties as New Location unless you change the name.)

Test Your Connection   Before you leave on your trip, change back to the original dialing properties and test your connection locally. If you don't have two phone lines, you might need to use your neighbor's or office-mate's. Don't assume that just because you connect successfully you can access the resources on your desktop PC. Test the Network Neighborhood to make sure you can access the shared resources.

Dialing Home When You're on the Road

Assuming your notebook and desktop PC are properly configured, establishing a remote connection is a breeze. Take the following steps:

1. Plug your notebook's modem into a phone jack.

2. Double-click My Computer.

3. Double-click Dial-Up Networking.

4. Double-click the Dial-Up Networking icon you created for dialing your desktop PC. The Connect To dialog box appears, as shown in Figure 14.7.

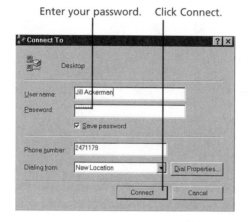

FIGURE 14.7   The Connect To dialog box prompts you to dial.

5. Type your password and click the Connect button.

6. When your desktop PC answers, double-click the Network Neighborhood icon on your Windows desktop to access your desktop PC's disks and folders. See Lesson 13, "Connecting Your Notebook and Desktop PCs," for instructions on how to navigate the Network Neighborhood.

Unable to Browse Network?   If you click the Entire Network icon and Windows displays a message indicating that you are unable to browse the network, highlight the entry in the Address text box and type the address to your desktop PC, for example, **\\Central**, and then press Enter. The address consists of two backslashes followed by the name you gave the desktop PC. To check (or change) the desktop PC's name, click the Network icon in the Control Panel and click the Identification tab. If you still have trouble displaying shared resources, check out Microsoft's technical support at www.microsoft.com or call (425) 635-7222.

When you are done using your desktop PC, disconnect to avoid additional phone charges. Right-click the Dial-Up Networking icon on the right end of the taskbar and click Disconnect.

This lesson showed you how to connect to your desktop PC or network via modem to access its resources when you're on the road. In the next lesson, you learn how to establish your Internet connection wherever you travel.

LESSON 15

Accessing Your Internet Connection on the Road

This lesson shows you how to connect to your ISP and keep track of your subscribed Web sites when you're on the road.

Because the Internet is a global communications network, staying connected when you're on the road might not pose a significant challenge. If your ISP provides a local access number for the area where you're staying, you simply create a new Dial-Up Networking connection for that number and you're ready to roll. You use the same technique if you sign up with an ISP that offers toll-free service.

However, there are a few issues that can make your Internet access less convenient than usual. This lesson addresses those issues and provides some tips for staying connected when you're on the road.

 Wireless Internet Connections   With a wireless PC card modem, you can establish an Internet connection without plugging into a phone jack. Appendix A, "Notebook Toys and Accessories," provides information about RIM's wireless PC card and GoAmerica's wireless Internet service. SpeedChoice (www.speedchoice.com) is another popular wireless ISP.

Finding Local and Toll-Free Internet Access Numbers

Most national ISPs offer toll-free access so that you can connect from anywhere in the country without paying long-distance fees. However, these "toll-free" numbers typically come with an hourly access fee of $4 to $6 per hour. Table 15.1 lists toll-free access numbers for the most popular ISPs. If your ISP is not listed, call customer service and ask about toll-free service.

TABLE 15.1   ISP Toll-Free Access Numbers

ISP	FEE	28.8KBPS	ISDN	56KBPS
AT&T WorldNet	$6/hour	800-543-3279	800-967-5363	800-967-5363
Concentric	$5/hour	800-991-4227	800-745-2747	800-745-2747
Earthlink	$4.95/hour	800-395-8410	800-395-8410	800-395-8410
GTE	$5.95/hour	800-638-1483	800-927-3000	800-927-3000
IBM	$6/hour	800-590-4857	800-821-4612	800-455-5056
MCI Internet	$5.95/hour	800-779-2966	800-348-8011	800-955-5210
MindSpring	N/A		800-719-4660	800-719-4660
Netcom	$4.90/hour	800-784-3638	888-316-1122	800-638-2661
Sprint	$4.80/hour	800-659-0090	800-786-1400	800-786-1400
SpryNet	$9/hour	800-572-1959	800-557-9614	800-557-9614

If you frequently travel and your ISP does not provide toll-free access, consider changing your ISP. Table 15.2 lists contact information for the most popular ISPs that offer toll-free access.

TABLE 15.2   ISPs That Offer Toll-Free Access

ISP	CALL	WEB SITE
A National ISP	800-262-3838	www.cisinternet.net
AT&T WorldNet	800-967-5363	www.att.net/worldnet/
Concentric	800-939-4262	www.concentric.com

ISP	CALL	WEB SITE
Earthlink	800-395-8425	www.earthlink.com
GTE	800-927-3000	www.gte.net
InfoNet	800-262-3838	www.annet.net
Internet Solutions	732-460-6600	www.telweb.com
MCI Internet	800-550-0927	www.mciworldcom.com
Netcom	800-638-2661	www.netcom.com
Norcom	561-392-2550	norcomld.com
Qwest	888-417-4414	www.netscape.com/qwest/isp
Sprint	800-359-3900	www.sprint.com/sip
Web-One	561-392-3999	www.web-one.com

Finding Local Access Numbers for Online Services

Most commercial online services, including America Online, CompuServe, and The Microsoft Network (MSN), offer nationwide service that provides local access numbers for most major cities. If your travels take you to an area where local access is unavailable, use the toll-free number for the service, as listed in Table 15.3. This table also shows you how to pull up access numbers online.

TABLE 15.3   Toll-Free Access Numbers for Commercial Online Services

SERVICE	FEE	TOLL-FREE	CALL FOR LOCAL NUMBERS	FIND INFORMATION ONLINE
America Online	$6/hour	800-716-0023	800-827-3338	Keyword access
CompuServe	$6/hour	800-331-7166	800-848-8990	Go phones

continues

TABLE 15.3   Continued

SERVICE	FEE	TOLL-FREE	CALL FOR LOCAL NUMBERS	FIND INFORMATION ONLINE
MSN	N/A	800-395-8410	800-386-5550	Connection Settings, Access Numbers
Prodigy	$.10/min	800-777-7997	800-776-3449	Go to www.prodigy.com, click Site Map, and click Access Numbers

To change the access number that your commercial online service uses to connect, consult its help system. For example, in America Online, you click the Setup button in the Welcome dialog box and then create or edit your location.

Changing the Access Number in Dial-Up Networking

If you changed ISPs or are setting up an Internet account for the first time on your notebook, you must create a new Dial-Up Networking connection, as explained in the following section. However, if you already set up a Dial-Up Networking connection for your ISP and merely need to use a different access number, the steps are much easier. When you're on the road and ready to get connected, take the following steps:

1. Double-click My Computer.

2. Double-click Dial-Up Networking.

3. Double-click the icon for connecting to your ISP. The Connect To dialog box appears, as shown in Figure 15.1.

4. Write down the number in the Phone Number text box so that you can change back to it later.

5. Highlight the number in the Phone Number text box and type the new local access number or toll-free number. (If you are entering a toll-free number, use only the last seven digits.)

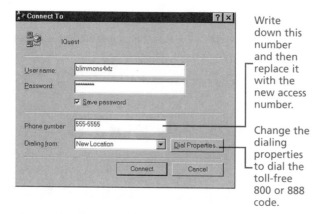

Write down this number and then replace it with the new access number.

Change the dialing properties to dial the toll-free 800 or 888 code.

FIGURE 15.1 You can quickly change the access number in the Connect To dialog box.

Remember to Set Your Modem's Dialing Properties Before you call from a remote location, check your modem's dialing properties, as explained in the section "Changing Your Modem's Dialing Properties" in Lesson 14. You might want to disable call waiting and might need to enter an access number for connecting to an outside line.

Keep Track of Access Numbers Use your word processor to keep a list of access numbers for the places you travel.

6. If you are using a toll-free number, click the Dial Properties button and proceed to step 7. If you are using a local number, skip to step 8.

7. Click in the Area Code text box and type the 800 or 888 code for the toll-free number and click OK.

8. If necessary, enter your username and password for logging on to the ISP. This should be the same name and password you use to connect from home base.

9. Click the Connect button.

Creating a New Dial-Up Networking Connection

If you travel all over the country or internationally, or if you changed ISPs, you must create a new Dial-Up Networking connection for the ISP. You might also want to create a new Dial-Up Networking icon for each place you visit. When you need to connect, you simply click the Dial-Up Networking icon for that area. Take the following steps to create a new Dial-Up Networking connection:

1. Open the Start menu, point to Programs, Internet Explorer, and click Connection Wizard.

2. Click the option button next to I Have an Existing Internet Account... and click Next. The Internet Connection Wizard now prompts you to specify the type of connection you want to set up.

3. Click the option button next to Select This Option If You Are Accessing the Internet Using an Internet Service Provider.... Click Next. You are now prompted to set up a new account.

4. If you are using a modem to connect, click Connect Using My Phone Line. If you are using a network connection, click Connect Using My Local Area Network (LAN). Click Next.

5. Click Create a New Dial-Up Connection and click Next.

6. If you are connecting via modem, enter the area code (or toll-free access code) in the Area Code text box and the phone number in the Telephone Number text box. Click Next.

7. Type your username in the User Name text box and then click in the Password text box and type your password. Click Next. You are now asked if you want to change the advanced settings.

Enter the Area Code   Although you might be connecting to a local number when you're on the road,
enter the area code, anyway. When you arrive at your
destination, you will change the dialing properties in
Windows to tell Windows your destination's area
code. Windows will then "know" that the number you
entered in step 6 is local and will skip the area code.

8. Click Yes so that you can check the settings before you continue.
   Click Next.

9. Choose the connection type specified by your service provider. If
   you're unsure, click PPP (Point to Point Protocol). Click Next.
   You are now asked to specify the type of logon procedure.

10. Most service providers enable Windows Dial-Up Networking to
    enter your name and password for you, so leave I Don't Need to
    Type Anything When Logging On selected. If your service
    provider requires you to log on manually or use a special logon
    script (usually supplied by the service provider), select the
    desired option. Click Next. The Internet Connection Wizard
    prompts you to enter your IP (Internet Protocol) address.

IP Address   The *IP (Internet Protocol)* address is a
number that identifies your computer on the Internet.

11. If your ISP assigns you an IP address when you log on (or if
    you're unsure), leave My Internet Service Provider
    Automatically Assigns Me One selected. If your ISP assigned
    you a permanent address, select Always Use the Following and
    type your address in the IP Address text box. Click Next.

12. If your service provider specified a DNS address, choose Always
    Use the Following and enter the DNS address in the DNS Server
    text box (see Figure 15.2). Click Next. You are now prompted to
    enter a name for the connection.

Use the Right Settings Your ISP should provide you with the required connection settings. If you have any questions regarding those settings, contact your ISP. A wrong guess can make it impossible to establish a connection or open Web pages.

Choose Always Use the Following.   Type the DNS server's address.   If your ISP has a second DNS server, enter its address here.

Internet Connection Wizard

DNS Server Address

Enter the Internet Protocol (IP) address of your DNS (Domain Name Service) server. You may specify an alternate server to try if the main DNS server is not available.

○ My Internet service provider automatically sets this when I sign in.

● Always use the following:

DNS server: 99.99.99.99

Alternate DNS server:

< Back   Next >   Cancel   Help

FIGURE 15.2 If your ISP provides a DNS server address, you must enter it.

13. Type a descriptive name for your ISP and click Next The Internet Connection Wizard asks if you want to set up your email account.

14. Click Yes, click Next, and follow the onscreen instructions to enter settings for your Internet email account. The Internet Connection Wizard asks if you want to set up your news server account.

15. Click Yes, click Next, and follow the onscreen instructions to set up a connection to the news server. The Internet Connection Wizard asks if you want to set up your directory service account.

16. Leave No selected and click Next. (You can set up a directory service later, if needed.) The Complete Configuration dialog box informs you that you have entered all the required information.

17. Click Finish.

Testing Your Connection

Never assume that an access number is correct or reliable. Before you leave on your trip, make sure you can use your new Dial-Up Networking icon to establish an Internet connection. (If you are dialing to a different area code, you must make a long-distance call to perform this test.) Take the following steps to check your connection:

1. Double-click My Computer.

2. Double-click Dial-Up Networking.

3. Double-click the Dial-Up Networking icon you created for connecting to your ISP.

4. Type your login name and password in the appropriate text boxes. To have Dial-Up Networking save your password, click Save Password to place a check mark in the box.

Don't Save Your Password   Because notebooks are so attractive to thieves, it's best to leave passwords off your notebook. You should also avoid storing any sensitive information on the notebook, such as credit card numbers.

5. Click the Connect button. Dial-Up Networking dials into the ISP and establishes a connection.

6. Test your Web browser and email programs to make sure they function properly over the connection.

If the connection fails or you cannot use your Web browser or email program over the connection, contact your ISP's technical support line. Make sure the connection works before you hit the road.

Dealing with Additional Connection Issues on the Road

When you arrive at your destination, you might not be able to establish a connection with the current dialing settings in Windows. The following list addresses the issues you must resolve:

- Change the dialing preferences in Windows to specify the area code of your current location. See the section "Changing Your Modem's Dialing Properties" in Lesson 14. If you don't specify the local area code, your modem might try to dial the area code you entered for your ISP even if you're connecting locally.

- Your modem typically waits for a dial tone before dialing out. If the phone system you're using has an odd dial tone or no dial tone, turn off dial-tone detection for your modem. In the Control Panel, double-click the Modems icon, click the modem you use, and click Properties Click the Connection tab and remove the check mark next to Wait for dial tone before dialing Click OK and then click Close

- If you turn off dial-tone detection and have trouble connecting, try typing two or three commas before the access number in the Connect To dialog box (for example, type ,,,555-5555). This tells your modem to wait a few seconds before dialing (each comma adds a wait time). If you're dialing a toll-free number, click the Dial Properties button and type the commas before the 888 or 800.

Accessing Subscribed Web Pages Via Email

If you subscribe to Web sites using the Web browser on your desktop PC, you can have your Web browser forward updated pages to your email account. This provides you with convenient access to your Web pages when you're away from your home or office.

To have Internet Explorer forward subscribed Web pages to an email address, take the following steps:

1. In Internet Explorer, open the Favorites menu and click Manage Subscriptions

2. Right-click the icon for the desired Web page and click Properties

3. Click the Receiving tab, as shown in Figure 15.3.

Click the
Receiving tab.

Make sure
this option
is selected.

Place a
check mark
next to this
option.

You can
specify the
email
address.

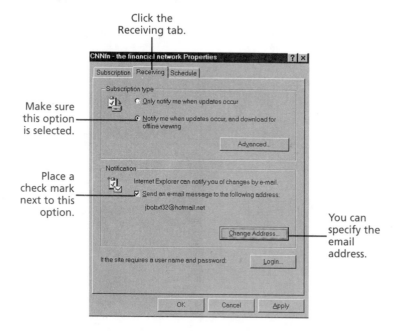

FIGURE 15.3 Change subscription settings for a Web page to have the page emailed to you.

4. Make sure there is a check mark next to Notify me when updates occur, and download for offline viewing

5. Click Send an email message to the following address

6. Click the Change Address button.

7. Type the email address to which you want the subscribed page sent.

8. In the Email server name (SMTP) text box, type the Internet mail server's address. This is usually "mail" or "smtp" followed by the domain name of the server. For example, if the domain name of your ISP's mail server were hotmail.net, you might type **mail.hotmail.net**

9. Click OK to return to the Properties dialog box.

10. Click OK to save your changes.

This lesson showed you how to stay connected to the Internet when you're on the road and have Internet Explorer email you subscribed Web pages. In the next lesson, you learn how use your notebook to stay in touch via email.

LESSON 16

Checking Your Email on the Road

This lesson shows you how to retrieve email from your online service, Internet account, and network when you're away from the office.

In the business world, email has become as essential for communications as the telephone. Email eliminates phone tag and enables you to keep a written log of your correspondence. In addition, it provides an efficient way to transmit documents and an inexpensive way to stay in touch with family when you're on a business trip.

However, when you're out of town, connecting to your email account poses some problems. Your Internet Service Provider (ISP) might not have a local number you can use to connect to your account. And if you receive email over a network connection at work, you must have some way to log on to the network and retrieve email remotely. This lesson addresses these problems and provides you with solutions and workarounds.

Retrieving Your Internet Email

Retrieving Internet email from a remote location is easy, assuming you have Outlook Express or another email program on your notebook. Before you leave, set up your email program by taking the following steps:

1. Contact your Internet Service Provider to determine whether the provider has a local number for that area or a toll-free number. Lesson 15, "Accessing Your Internet Connection on the Road," provides information on how to obtain these numbers for the most popular ISPs.

2. If your ISP does have a local or toll-free number, set up a new Dial-Up Networking connection for that number, as explained in Lesson 15.

3. Test the new connection to make sure you can connect using that number. (This might consist of dialing long distance.)

4. Configure the Telephony settings in Windows to specify the location and area code for the geographical location where you'll be. See "Changing Your Modem's Dialing Properties," in Lesson 14, "Remote Computing Via Modem," for instructions.

After you set up your modem to dial into your ISP and establish a connection, the process for sending and receiving email is the same no matter where you travel.

Retrieving Email from Your Network

When you're leaving on a trip, do you ask an officemate to check your email? Do you really trust a coworker to rummage through your messages? You don't have to. With the proper software, you can manage your email from your remote location.

 pcANYWHERE   You can use a remote computing program such as pcANYWHERE to use any of the programs on your desktop PC, including the email program. For details about pcANYWHERE and to download a trial version, visit www.symantec.com/pca/.

Working with Your Network or Email Administrator

In order to retrieve network email from a remote location, you must contact the network or email administrator for help. You must use a remote email program that can access the specific type of email server your organization uses. For example, you cannot use cc:Mail to access email on a Microsoft Exchange server or use Outlook to access mail on a cc:Mail server. In addition, your organization must have one or more modems connected to the mail server to support access via modem. The administrator will be able to provide you with the following information:

- Your username and password.

- The post office or mail server name.

- The phone number your modem needs to use to dial in.

Seeing How It's Done with cc:Mail Mobile

To understand how remote email access works, let's look at an example using cc:Mail Mobile. With cc:Mail Mobile, you log on to the cc:Mail server using your modem and download your messages. You can then read and reply to those messages just as if you were sitting at your main PC. The following steps show you how to set up cc:Mail Mobile:

1. Open the Start menu, point to Programs, Lotus Applications, and click Lotus cc:Mail Mobile.

2. Type your login name and password and click OK. The Lotus cc:Mail Mobile dialog box appears, indicating that no post office was found and asking if you want to create a new one.

3. Click OK.

4. Type post office or mail server name in the PO Name text box and type any additional notes in the Comment text box. This name must match exactly the name as specified by your administrator (see Figure 16.1).

5. Leave the Address Type set to Phone.

6. If necessary, open the Country drop-down list and choose the country in which the post office (network mail server) is located.

7. In the Area/City Code text box, type the area code you must dial to connect to the post office.

8. In the Local Number text box, type the post office's phone number.

9. Click the Add button.

10. Click OK. The Edit Communication Method dialog box appears.

Type post office or
mail server name.

Make sure Address
Type is set to Phone.

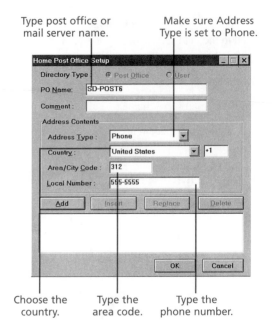

Choose the
country.

Type the
area code.

Type the
phone number.

FIGURE 16.1   Enter the phone settings for connecting to your
email post office (the network mail server).

11. Choose your modem type and specify the desired speaker volume, as shown in Figure 16.2, and then click OK. Do not change
the COM port or modem speed settings unless you have trouble
establishing a connection.

When you successfully set up your email program for remote email, the
process for retrieving messages is the same as in any email program. For
example, in cc:Mail Mobile, you open the Mobile menu and choose
Receive Mail. cc:Mail Mobile connects to the mail server and downloads
your messages, as shown in Figure 16.3. You can then disconnect and read
your messages offline.

Choose a
speaker volume.

Select your
modem.

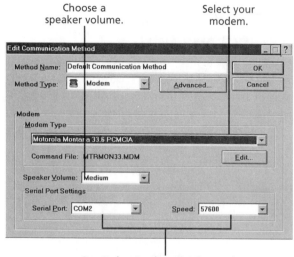

FIGURE 16.2   Enter your modem settings.

Don't change these settings unless
you have trouble connecting.

List of received messages

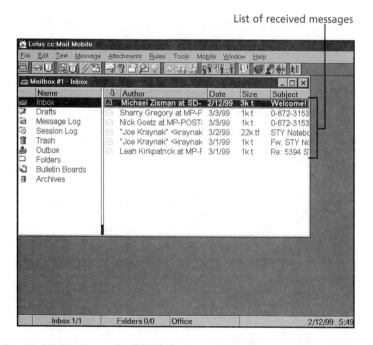

FIGURE 16.3   Use cc:Mail Mobile to retrieve messages directly from
your network's mail server when you're on a trip.

Forwarding Messages to a More Convenient Account

One of the easiest ways to make sure you receive all your email messages when you're away from the office is to have your main PC forward your messages to your Internet account. The following steps provide an example of how to forward messages with Outlook Express:

1. Open the Tools menu and choose Inbox Assistant

2. Click the Add button.

3. At the top of the Properties dialog box, click the check box next to All Messages (see Figure 16.4).

4. Click the check box next to Forward to

5. Click in the Forward to text box and type your Internet email address.

6. Click OK.

Click Forward to.   Click All Messages.   Type the email address to which you want messages forwarded.

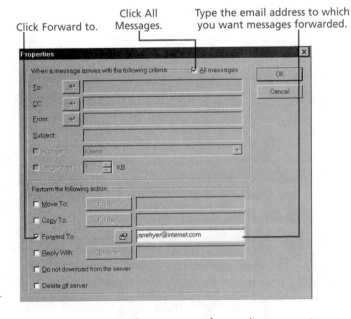

FIGURE 16.4   Tell your email program to forward messages to a more convenient account.

Reading Your Messages Offline

To reduce long-distance charges or hourly Internet fees, retrieve your mail and then disconnect and read it offline. Use your email program's offline features to compose messages offline. You can then connect, quickly send the messages, and log off.

The procedure for setting these options varies depending on the email program you're using. The following steps show you how to set the options in Outlook Express:

1. Open the Tools menu and click Options.

2. Click the Send tab.

3. Click the check box next to Send messages immediately to remove the check mark. This tells Outlook Express to place the messages in the Outbox until you click the Send and Receive button.

4. Click the Dial Up tab.

5. Click the check box next to Hang up when finished sending, receiving or downloading (see Figure 16.5).

6. Click OK.

 Use Remote Mail   Many advanced email programs such as Microsoft Outlook include a remote mail feature. Such a feature downloads the message headers (descriptions), enabling you to download the contents of only those messages you want to read.

Click this option.

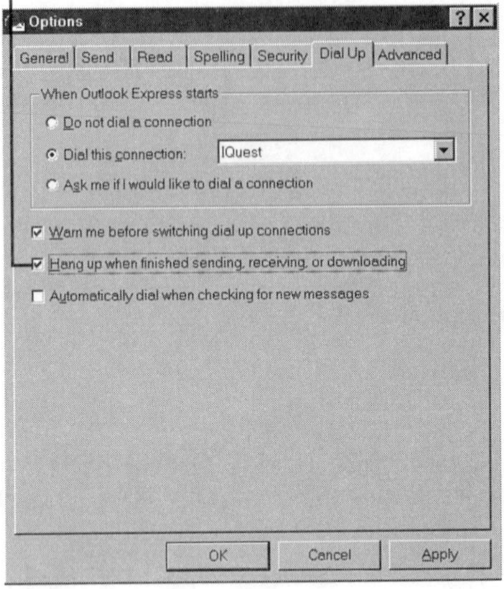

FIGURE 16.5 Tell your email program to automatically hang up when it is done receiving or sending messages.

This lesson showed you how to retrieve your email from a network when you're away on a trip. In the next lesson, you learn how to use your notebook to give business presentations.

Lesson 17

Taking Your Business Presentations on the Road

This lesson shows you how to use your notebook along with some fancy peripherals to make your business presentations portable.

Notebooks are not only useful for taking a little work home from the office or performing some light editing on the road. Their portability also makes them ideal for carrying presentations into boardrooms wherever you travel.

However, showing up at a client's company in the hopes that the sales presentation stored on your notebook will go off without a hitch is a bit much to expect. You must prepare well in advance and be able to deal with any technical difficulties you might encounter.

Essential Presentation Peripherals

The days of 35mm slide shows and overhead transparencies are coming to an end. Sales people, trainers, and educators commonly display their slide shows electronically, using projectors and speaker systems to display slide shows that include animated text and transitions, video clips, audio clips, and other media.

Notebooks make it convenient to carry your presentation with you, assuming your notebook is equipped with the required output devices:

- **Projector**   The key to any presentation is the projector (see
  Figure 17.1). To use a projector with your notebook, you must
  connect it to the VGA port on your notebook. Before giving
  your presentation, make sure you have the correct driver loaded
  for the projector. See the following section, "Connecting a
  Projector," for details. (If your notebook has a Video Out port,
  you can choose to display your presentation on a TV screen, as
  explained later in this lesson.)

FIGURE **17.1** A portable projector enables your notebook to display
professional presentations on the road. (Photo courtesy of Kodak.)

 Sticker Shock If you think your notebook was over-
priced, you'll be shocked when you start shopping for
a portable projector. A good, portable projector can
cost over $6,000!

- **Remote pointer**   If you're standing in front of an audience, you
  can't use your mouse to navigate. Here's where a wireless mouse
  comes in handy. The control that comes with most projectors
  includes buttons for controlling the mouse pointer. If you need to
  type during your presentation, you can also purchase remote
  keyboards.

- **Speaker system**   For presentations that include music, narration, or other audio, make sure your sound system is up to the task. You don't want to play audio through the dinky speakers on your notebook. Most projectors have built-in audio that's much better than your notebook's audio system.

- **Cables and power cords**   When you're walking into an unfamiliar room to give a presentation, make sure you have a long extension cord and the cables needed to set up your projector and audio system. Also, make sure you have the AC adapter for your notebook; don't count on battery power for the entire presentation.

- **Duct tape**   Bring duct tape or wide masking tape for taping down any loose cords so that no one will trip on them.

- **Presentation backup**   Although your presentation will run best from your notebook's hard drive, carry a backup on a CD-ROM disc or Zip disk. If anything happens to the original presentation file, you can use the backup.

Invest in a CD-RW Drive   A CD-Read/Write drive can transfer data to a CD as well as read CDs. If you're in the business of taking presentations on the road, consider adding a CD-RW drive to your main system.

Retrofit Your Overhead Projector   You can purchase a flat LCD display that lays on top of an overhead projector screen. The overhead projector passes light through the display to project images, including slide shows, spreadsheets, and anything else you can run or open on your notebook.

Connecting a Projector

Connecting a projector to your notebook is as easy as connecting an external monitor. However, the projector might come with some additional equipment, such as built-in speakers to provide enhanced sound and an infrared pointer you can use as a remote control. To hook up your projector and any additional equipment, take the following steps:

1. Shut down your notebook and turn off the power to your notebook and the projector.

2. Plug one end of the cable into the VGA port on your notebook, as shown in Figure 17.2.

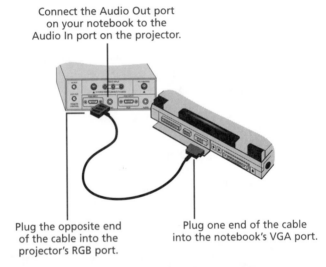

Connect the Audio Out port
on your notebook to the
Audio In port on the projector.

Plug the opposite end
of the cable into the
projector's RGB port.

Plug one end of the cable
into the notebook's VGA port.

FIGURE 17.2   Connect the projector to your notebook's VGA port.

3. Connect the other end of the cable into the RGB port on the projector.

 RGB   Short for *Red Green Blue*, *RGB* is a display technology that requires a separate signal for each color. Color monitors and most projectors use this technology.

4. If the projector has built-in audio, plug one end of the audio cable into the Audio Out port on your notebook.

5. Plug the opposite end of the cable into the Audio In port on the projector.

6. If the projector came with a remote control for the mouse, plug the infrared or radio-frequency adapter into the mouse or serial port on your notebook. Refer to the documentation that came with the projector for details.

7. Turn on the projector, speakers, and your notebook.

8. If the projector and your notebook support Plug and Play, the Add New Hardware Wizard will appear on startup and lead you through the process of installing the driver for the projector and, if present, remote control. If the Add New Hardware Wizard does not start, open the Control Panel and double-click the Add New Hardware icon.

9. Follow the onscreen instructions to install the driver(s) that came with the projector.

Most notebooks have a special key combination you must press in order to toggle between the built-in display, VGA output, or both. See Lesson 4, "Navigating the Streamlined Keyboard," for details.

 Getting Fancy Most projectors also have input jacks for other audio/video equipment. For example, you can connect a VCR player to the projector to play video clips during the presentation.

Displaying Your Presentation on a TV Screen

If you plan on giving a presentation to a small group of people who will be sitting fairly close to you, you might be able to do without an expensive projector. Assuming your notebook has a composite video out port or S-video jacks, you can connect your notebook to a standard television set (via its composite video or S-video in jack) to play your presentation.

Video Adapters Make sure you have the video adapters you need to connect to the TV set. Most notebooks have an S-video out jack that you must connect to the composite video in jack on the TV, which requires a special adapter to make the connection. You can pick up such an adapter at most stores that sell consumer electronics equipment.

To connect your notebook to a TV set, take the following steps:

1. Shut down your notebook and turn off the power to your notebook and the TV set.

2. Plug one end of the video cable into the Video Out jack on your notebook, as shown in Figure 17.3.

S-video jack on notebook.

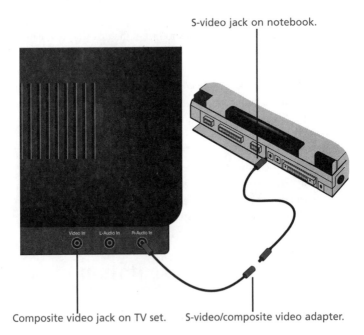

Composite video jack on TV set.   S-video/composite video adapter.

FIGURE **17.3**   A TV provides an affordable way to display your presentations.

3. Plug the connector on the opposite end of the cable into the composite video or S-video in connector on the TV.

Use the Correct TV Jack   Most TV sets have two or three input jacks that look similar: one for composite video input and one or two for audio input (two if the TV set has stereo output). Make sure you connect to the composite video input jack.

4. Turn on the TV and the notebook. Your notebook should automatically send video output to both the TV and the notebook's monitor.

No Video Out Jack?   If you don't have a Video Out jack on your notebook, you can purchase a device that converts VGA output into TV output, and it costs much less than a video projector. Check out AVerMedia's AVerKey 300 at www.averkey.com.

Preparing to Give Your Presentation

Preparation is the key to success. Before giving your presentation, take the following steps to prepare:

- Rehearse your presentation thoroughly with the equipment you plan to use. If your remote pointer doesn't quite work like the documentation says it does, your audience will not be impressed.

- Adjust the display resolution for maximum clarity from the projector. See Lesson 6, "Changing Your Notebook's Display Settings," for details. You might need to tweak the color scheme in your presentation.

- If possible, set up and test your equipment the day before you give the presentation.

- Adjust the focus on your projector and make sure the projector lens is pointing directly at the screen or wall.

- Connect, position, and tape down all cords and cables.

- If you have a screen saver on your notebook, turn it off. Also turn off any power-conservation utilities. You don't want your screen blanking out in the middle of a presentation. See Lesson 7, "Conserving Battery Power," for instructions on configuring the power-conservation utilities.

 Place It on the Desktop   To make accessing your presentation file convenient, use the right mouse button to drag the icon from My Computer over a blank area of the Windows desktop. Release the mouse button and click Create Shortcut(s) Here. When you're ready to run the presentation, just double-click its shortcut.

This lesson showed you how to prepare your notebook to give business presentations on the road. In the next lesson, you learn how to use a global positioning device to find your way around the country.

LESSON 18
Navigating the Highways Via Satellite

This lesson shows you how to connect a global positioning device to your notebook and use it to guide you from your current location to a desired destination.

Map programs such as AutoMap have been around for years, helping people find the quickest or most scenic route to their destination. With a map program, you plot your starting point and destination and the program highlights the highways and byways you must take to get there.

A relatively new navigational device, called a global positioning system (GPS for short), has added its expertise to map programs. A GPS receives satellite signals and feeds them through your notebook to the map program. The program then pinpoints your exact location on the map to help you determine where you are and where you need to turn. Most global positioning systems even provide spoken directions, telling you when your next turn is coming up!

No Extra Fees Required You don't have to subscribe to a satellite service. The United States Department of Defense (DOD) manages the satellites used for GPS navigation. For security purposes, the satellite signals provide less accurate positioning for public use than they are capable of providing for the defense system. Your GPS should be able to determine your position within 100 meters.

Popular Global Positioning Systems

If your work requires you to drive to obscure locations in your city or state or around the country, you might need the assistance of a navigator. The following is a list of the most popular global positioning systems on the market:

> *CoPilot* from TravRoute (www.travroute.com) is an in-car navigation system that gives you audio instructions. You specify your desired destination and CoPilot determines your current location, calculates the fastest route from your location to the destination, and *tells* you how to get there. CoPilot is featured in this lesson to illustrate how to use a global positioning system.

> *Earthmate* by Delorme (www.delorme.com) is similar to CoPilot, providing onscreen and audio directions to your destination. Earthmate comes with Street Atlas USA for mapping your route.

> *Garmin GPS III* by Garmin International (www.garmin.com) is a standalone GPS receiver that you can connect to your notebook with an optional cable. Gamin's products are for the more avid world traveler. And if you're in the market for a new fish finder, Garmin's the place to go.

Installing Your Global Positioning System

You might think that installing a GPS would be complicated. In fact, it's as easy as installing a serial mouse. Take the following steps:

1. Shut down Windows and turn off the power to your notebook.

2. Connect the GPS receiver to your notebook as the GPS documentation instructs. CoPilot requires two cable connections: one cable plugs into the PS/2 port or cigarette lighter (for power) and the other plugs into the serial port (for data transfer) (see Figure 18.1).

Serial port   Connection to PS/2 port

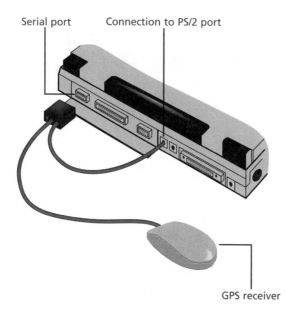

GPS receiver

FIGURE 18.1 Most GPS receivers connect to the serial port.

3. Insert the map software CD into your notebook's CD-ROM drive. If AutoPlay is on, your notebook plays the CD and initiates the setup program.

4. If the setup program does not start, use the Start, Run command to run the Setup or Install file on the CD.

5. Follow the onscreen instructions to install the map software on your notebook's hard drive (see Figure 18.2).

6. If the program requires a separate installation of the speech software, perform that installation as instructed.

7. Stick the GPS receiver to the dashboard of your car and drive to a relatively open area. (The receiver can't receive a satellite signal if you're setting this up in your home or if the car is parked in a garage or under a tree.)

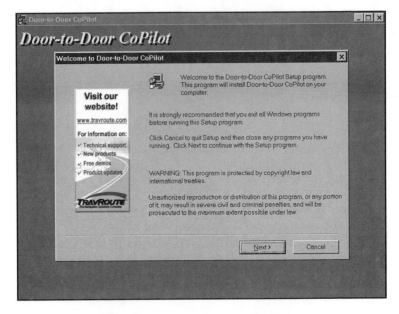

FIGURE **18.2** Follow the onscreen setup instructions to install the map software.

 Clear View of the Sky Required In order for the satellite receiver to pick up signals, the receiver needs a clear view of the sky. If tall buildings or trees are in the way, they can block the required signals. In addition, the first time you use the receiver, it might take several minutes to pick up the satellite signals.

Specifying Your Destination

In a standard map program, you specify your current location and desired destination and the map program highlights the route. With GPS, the receiver automatically determines your current location, so you simply enter your destination. Take the following steps to specify your destination:

1. Start your GPS program.

2. If the program does not prompt you for your destination, enter the command for starting a new trip. A dialog box appears asking for your desired destination (see Figure 18.3).

Enter a city, place, or ZIP code.   Enter a specific address.

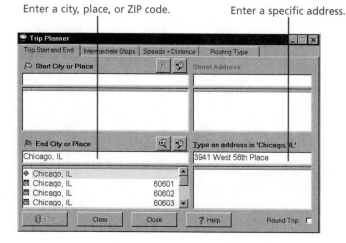

FIGURE 18.3   The GPS program prompts you to specify the desired destination.

3. In the destination text box, type the city and state or ZIP code of the desired destination. If your destination is a park, landmark, or other popular place, enter its name.

4. For a more precise destination, enter the street address.

5. Click the Run button or enter the equivalent command to have the program plot your route. The program highlights the route, as shown in Figure 18.4.

Destination

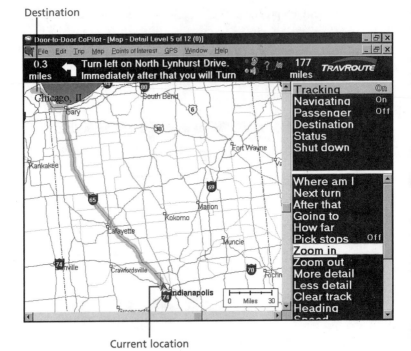

Current location

FIGURE **18.4** The program automatically plots the shortest route from your current position to your destination.

Talking with Your CoPilot

As you drive along, the GPS keeps track of your ever-changing location and displays your progress on the map, as shown in Figure 18.5. If the program has voice capabilities, it gives you verbal instructions to let you know when your next turn is coming up. With CoPilot, if you decide to take a detour or you make a wrong turn, CoPilot re-routes you, informs you that it is "recalculating the route," and provides new directions.

Departure point   Current location   Destination

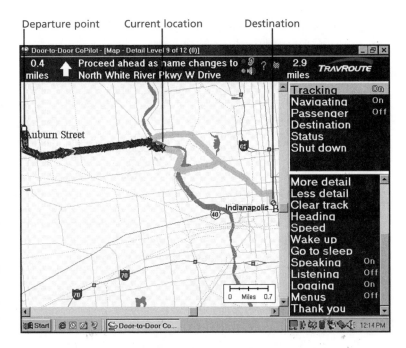

FIGURE 18.5 CoPilot displays arrow icons to show your progress as you near your destination.

Some GPS programs, including CoPilot, can accept voice commands, as well, assuming your car is fairly quiet. You can ask questions such as "How far?" and "Which way?" and the GPS program answers back. However, this works better if you have a quality microphone attached to the audio input and position the microphone near your mouth. In any case, speak slowly and clearly.

Before you leave for your destination, crank up the audio on your notebook. Also turn up the audio in Windows by taking the following steps:

1. Double-click the speaker icon on the right end of the taskbar.

2. Open the Options menu and choose Properties.

3. Under Show the following volume controls, place a check mark next to every option except PC Speaker and then click OK.

4. Make sure none of the volume controls has a check mark in its Mute box.

5. Drag the Volume Control, Wave, and Microphone Volume controls to the top.

6. Click OK.

If the volume is too loud, try adjusting it with the notebook's external control or perform these steps again to lower the volume. On most notebooks, you'll want the volume as loud as possible so that you can hear the directions as you drive.

Keep Your Eyes on the Road   When driving with a GPS, it's tempting to peek at the screen. To avoid accidents, concentrate on driving. If you must look at the screen, pull your car off the road first.

Your GPS Is Not Always Right   Due to the complexity of street systems across the United States, the fact that the GPS receiver is accurate to only 100 meters, and the inevitable traffic construction and road closings, the program might not always give you the most accurate or efficient directions, but it'll usually get you where you're going. Use your own common sense when listening to your co-pilot.

Other Cool GPS Features

Although a GPS is great for finding your way from point A to point B, it typically provides additional features that are both useful and fun. Here are some of the cool things you can do:

*   **Find out how long it will take**   If you're wondering how long it's going to take you to drive to the specified destination, your GPS provides an estimated time. In addition, you can choose to have your GPS determine the fastest route, which is not necessarily the shortest.

- **Make a list of favorite places**   If you commonly travel to a particular place, you can mark it as one of your favorite places and then select it from a list. You don't have to enter the city and address every time.

- **Find motels, restaurants, and points of interest**   The database included with your GPS should have an extensive list of motels, restaurants, parks, and recreational areas. If you like to wander the country but don't want to miss anything, the GPS can point you in the right direction. Check with the GPS manufacturer to determine whether database updates and additional travel databases are available.

- **Find out how fast you're going**   Although your speedometer provides a better indication of your car's speed, you can double-check your speed against the GPS.

- **Mark blocked streets**   You can mark streets that are closed or being repaired and the GPS will route you around those streets.

- **Mark intermediate stops**   Mark your destination and all points between your current location and your destination to have your GPS route each leg of the trip.

- **Check your coordinates**   You can check your precise longitudinal and latitudinal coordinates...just in case you're wondering where on earth you ended up.

- **Get Internet feedback**   Most GPS manufacturers have a Web site for registered users that includes information about travel conditions and weather for most major cities.

This lesson showed you how to use a global positioning device in tandem with your notebook to find your way around the country. In the next lesson, you learn how to talk face-to-face with people over the telephone or an Internet connection.

LESSON 19

Videoconfer-encing with Your Notebook

This lesson shows you how to connect a digital video camera to your notebook and talk face-to-face with clients over a phone line or Internet connection.

With faster modems and the availability of affordable, high-quality video cameras, videoconferencing over network and Internet connections is becoming more and more popular. You can now talk to people all over the world in real time without paying long-distance charges, assuming, of course, that you and the other person have the proper equipment and software.

Obtaining the Required Videoconferencing Hardware

To videoconference successfully, the most important component is a high-speed connection. If your system has a 28.8Kbps modem and a half-duplex audio system, audio and video signals will crawl through the lines. The following list describes the standard hardware you should have for reasonable videoconferencing performance:

- **V.80 modem**   You need a video-enabled V.80 modem (33.6K or 56K) or ISDN adapter. (V.80 is a modem standard for videoconferencing.) The modem should support both H.323 and H.324 standards. These standards help ensure that two people using different videoconferencing hardware can successfully connect. H.323 governs videoconferencing over the Internet and network connections. H.324 governs videoconferencing via POTS (plain old telephone system) using an analog modem and has generated the latest wave of consumer-based videoconferencing products.

- **Full-duplex audio**   A full-duplex audio system can process audio input and output at the same time, providing for smooth transitions while you and the other person talk. A half-duplex audio system can do only one thing at a time: input audio or output audio. If you try to carry on a normal conversation (without long pauses), half duplex will drive you up a wall.

- **Speakers and microphone**   The audio system generates the audio output through the speakers and receives input from a microphone. Consider purchasing a headset or a microphone that clips onto your lapel to place the microphone closer to your mouth. Your notebook's built-in microphone might pick up a lot of background noise.

- **Powerful processor**   Most videoconferencing kits recommend 150MHz or 166MHz systems because the processor is in charge of handling data compression.

- **Parallel, USB, or video capture port**   The video camera requires a connection to the parallel port, a USB port, or a video capture port. If you have a camera that requires a video capture port, you might need to install a video capture PC card.

- **Video camera**   The video camera "films" you during the conference.

 Using a Camcorder   You need not use a special video camera for PCs. If your notebook has a video capture port (or PC card), you can connect a camcorder to the port.

Shopping for Videoconferencing Equipment

When shopping for videoconferencing equipment, first consider the limitations of your system. If you have a 56Kbps modem or slower, shopping for a camera that spits out 30 frames per second makes little sense; the modem will choke at that rate. With that in mind, here are the most important features to consider when shopping for videoconferencing equipment:

- **Camera resolution**   Expect maximum resolutions of 620×240. Lower resolution cameras produce small, low-quality graphics. Higher resolution cameras produce large graphics that can slow down communications.

- **Frames per second**   Opt for a videoconferencing package that offers 15fps (frames per second). Some systems attain smooth video with less than 15fps, but don't purchase a camera that operates at less than 10fps. (Depending on your modem, you might be lucky to see 5fps during a call.)

- **Lighting adjustments**   Most videoconferencing cameras enable you to adjust the lighting and focus by using software controls. A higher-end camera might provide controls for adjusting the camera itself. Lower-end products might provide no controls, forcing you to manually adjust the lighting in the room.

- **Videoconferencing software**   For videoconferencing over the Internet or across network connections, Microsoft's NetMeeting (www.microsoft.com), Netscape's Conference (www.netscape.com/download/), and White Pine Software's CU-SeeMe (www.wpine.com) lead the pack. For modem-to-modem videoconferencing, most videoconferencing kits include third-party software from VDOnet (www.vdo.net), Smith Micro Software (www.smithmicro.com), or Intel (www.intel.com).

The following is a list of the more popular videoconferencing kits, along with a brief description of each:

QuickCam VC   Logitech has bundled its popular QuickCam desktop video camera with its VideoPhone software to create this videoconferencing kit. QuickCam VC supports both the H.323 and H.324 standards for Internet and modem-to-modem videoconferencing. For details, go to www.quickcam.com. You'll need a full-duplex audio system and a 28.8Kbps modem (for Internet use) or V.80 modem for modem-to-modem connections. If you have a USB port, get the USB version. The parallel port version requires parallel and PS/2 port connections.

EggCam   Panasonic's EggCam is an egg-shaped digital camera that plugs into a video capture port. To use it, your notebook must have video capture capabilities or you must add a PC card video capture board. You can try to find information about the product at www.panasonic.com.

PAR Kritter Kam   One of the few videoconferencing cameras designed specifically for notebooks, the PAR Kritter Kam clips on to the notebook's case (see Figure 19.1). However, the Kritter Kam requires the addition of a video capture PC card (preferably the PAR CapSure, which requires a Zoomed Video Port). Check out these products at www.partec.com.

©1999 PAR Technologies

FIGURE **19.1**   Kritter Kam is a high-performance video camera designed specifically for notebooks. (Photo courtesy of PAR Technologies.)

   Zoomed Video Port   *Zoomed Video Port* is a PCMCIA standard for PC cards that enables the video capture PC card to communicated directly with the VGA controller. This improves video performance by enabling the video data to bypass the processor.

USB Cameras Steal the Show   If you have a USB port, look for a USB video camera. USB cameras are typically less expensive and perform better than cameras that connect to the parallel port. In addition, they require only one cable connection. Parallel port cameras require a connection to the parallel port and to a PS/2 port or AC adapter.

Choosing a Videoconferencing Connection

There are three ways to videoconference: over the Internet, over a network connection, or by way of a modem-to-modem connection:

- To conference over the Internet, you log on to a central server, which displays a list of people you can call. You select the person from the directory or enter the person's logon name or email address. With your videoconferencing setup, you can talk to the other person and send live video. If the other person has a digital video camera, you can see the person. Otherwise, you receive only audio. (See the step-by-step instructions in the following section.)

- Videoconferencing over network lines is similar to videoconferencing over the Internet. You can even use the same videoconferencing software, such as Microsoft NetMeeting. The two main differences are that the connection is much faster and you place your call by typing the person's network logon name or the name of the person's computer.

- Modem-to-modem videoconferencing is a more private affair. You use your modem and videoconferencing software to dial another person's modem directly. Assuming the other person's modem answers the phone (and both systems use compatible software), you can talk face-to-face.

Using NetMeeting to Videoconference Over the Internet

The steps you must take to initiate a videoconferencing connection vary depending on the program you use. To get a feel for what's involved in videoconferencing, the following sections lead you through the process of using Microsoft NetMeeting to place a call over the Internet. Because NetMeeting is included with Internet Explorer, you might want to perform the steps to get some hands-on experience.

Setting Up NetMeeting

Before you can use NetMeeting to place a call, you must set up NetMeeting and make sure your videoconferencing hardware is working properly. Take the following steps to set up NetMeeting:

1. Click the Start button, point to Programs, Internet Explorer, and click Microsoft NetMeeting.

2. Click Next.

3. Open the directory server list and choose the ILS (Internet Locator Server) that the people you want to call will be using. (If you're not sure, leave the current selection.) Click Next. NetMeeting prompts you to enter information about yourself.

 ILS   An *ILS* is a telephone directory for NetMeeting. You can open the ILS to view a list of people who are connected to a specific ILS server. To call the person, you select his or her name from the list. Without the ILS, you have to enter a person's email address in order to call the person.

4. Type the requested information. The First Name, Last Name, and E-Mail Address entries are required. Click Next.

5. Click the option that best describes how you intend to use NetMeeting: personal, business, or adults-only use. Click Next. NetMeeting prompts you to specify your connection type.

6. Choose your modem speed or ISDN (if you are using an ISDN modem), or, if you are using NetMeeting on a network, choose Local Area Network. Click Next. NetMeeting prompts you to choose the video capture device you want to use (see Figure 19.2).

FIGURE 19.2   NetMeeting prompts you to choose the video capture device.

7. Assuming you have only one video capture device installed, click Next. NetMeeting connects to the server and displays a list of people currently connected. You can now place a call. NetMeeting displays a message telling you to close any programs that record or play audio.

8. Close any programs, as needed, and click Next. The Audio Tuning Wizard appears.

9. Click the Test button to make sure your sound card and speakers are working. NetMeeting sounds a beep. If the beep is too loud or too soft, drag the Volume slider to adjust the volume. Click Next. The wizard displays a bar showing the recording volume.

10. Speak in to your microphone while watching the bar. The bar should expand to the right as you speak. If the bar does not

extend past the halfway mark, use the Record Volume slider to increase the volume. Click Next. The wizard indicates that you have successfully set up NetMeeting.

11. Click Finish.

Placing a Videoconference Call

After you set up NetMeeting and adjust the volume controls, you can place a call. Take the following steps:

1. Click the Directory icon in NetMeeting's Navigation bar.

2. Open the Server drop-down list and select the ILS you want to use to find people. NetMeeting logs on to the server and displays a list of all the people on the server (see Figure 19.3). If a red asterisk appears in the left column, the person is already participating in a call. Additional icons indicate whether the person is using an audio or video connection.

FIGURE 19.3   NetMeeting displays a list of people currently logged on to the server you selected.

3. To filter the list, you can choose an option from the Category drop-down list. For example, you can choose to view a list of only those people who are not participating in a call.

4. Scroll down the list and double-click the person's name or right-click the person's name and select Call. When you place a call, a dialog box pops up on the screen of the person you called and the person's computer "rings." Assuming the person you called wants to talk with you, she clicks the Accept button and you can start talking (see Figure 19.4).

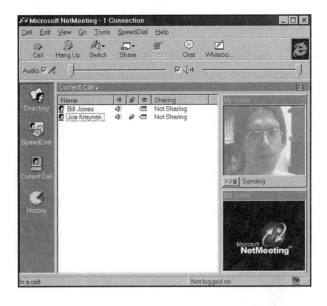

FIGURE **19.4**   After you are connected, you can start talking.

5. To adjust the display, choose Tools, Options, click the Video tab, and enter your preferences (see Figure 19.5).

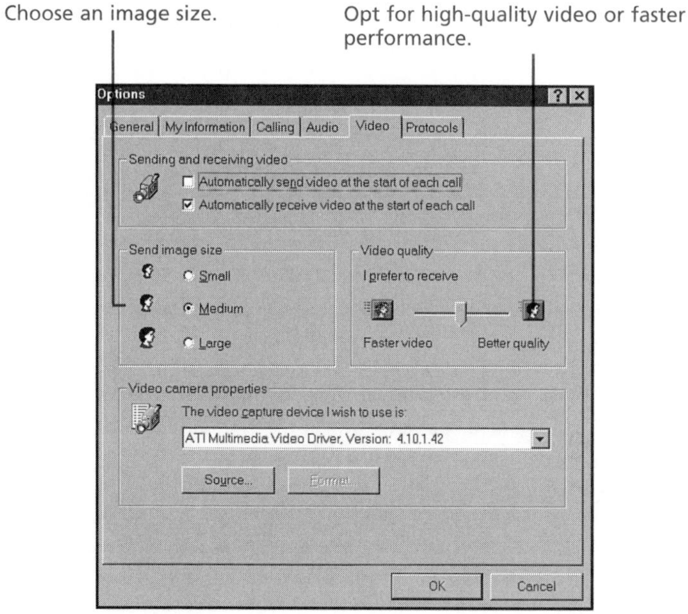

Choose an image size.   Opt for high-quality video or faster performance.

FIGURE 19.5   You can enter preferences to increase the speed or quality of the video you send and receive.

6. Click the Source button to adjust the image brightness and color. Enter your preferences for brightness, contrast, color, and tint.

7. When you finish talking, click the Hang Up button in the toolbar.

This lesson showed you how to videoconference with your notebook. In the next lesson, you learn how to keep your notebook in top operating condition.

LESSON 20

Maintaining Your Notebook

This lesson shows you how to keep your notebook running in top operating condition.

When you think of notebook maintenance, you might have visions of wiping off the screen and vacuuming around the ventilation holes. Although it's important to keep your notebook clean, you must also maintain Windows and the files stored on your notebook's hard disk. This lesson shows you how to maintain your notebook inside and out.

Keeping Your Notebook Clean

Although your notebook might appear to house all its components in a hermetically sealed case, the fact is your notebook is a dust magnet. To clean your notebook, first shut down Windows and turn off the power. Then perform the following tasks:

- Using a brush attachment for your vacuum cleaner, vacuum the notebook's keyboard. Vacuum the case, especially around the ventilation holes and ports, being very careful not to bend any pins.

- Using a cloth *slightly* dampened with distilled water, wipe the monitor. The cloth should be damp, not dripping; you don't want water to seep between the monitor and the case.

- If your notebook has a touchpad, use the same cloth to wipe any dust or dirt off the touchpad. Use a dry cotton swab to remove any dust from around the edges.

Use a Dryer Sheet A *used* dryer sheet is excellent for wiping dust off the monitor. Dryer sheets are anti-static and can actually prevent future dust build-up. Don't use a new dryer sheet, though, because the chemicals in it will streak the screen.

Running the Windows Maintenance Wizard

Windows 98 includes the Maintenance Wizard, which automatically performs several maintenance tasks on your notebook at scheduled times. Maintenance Wizard runs the following utilities at the times you specify:

Disk Cleanup clears useless files from your hard disk, including temporary files created and never deleted by applications, Internet files, any files in the Recycle Bin, and Windows 98 uninstall files (if you upgraded from Windows 95).

Disk Defragmenter optimizes the arrangement of files on your hard disk, making it easier for your notebook to find and load files.

ScanDisk scans for and fixes disk errors and attempts to find and recover damaged files.

In addition, Maintenance Wizard displays a list of programs that are set up to automatically run on startup and enables you to prevent them from running automatically to streamline the Windows startup.

Run the Utilities Separately Although the Maintenance Wizard is an excellent tool for desktop PCs that run constantly, it is less practical on a notebook that is typically turned off after each use. If you choose to use Maintenance Wizard, schedule your system tune-ups for times when your notebook is typically plugged in but when you are not actively using it. If you choose not to use Maintenance Wizard, later sections in this lesson show you how to run the utilities separately.

To run the Windows Maintenance Wizard, take the following steps:

1. Choose Start, Programs, Accessories, System Tools, Maintenance Wizard.

2. Click Custom and then click Next.

3. Choose Nights, Days, or Evenings and click Next.

4. To have Windows start faster, remove the check mark next to any programs that you do not want to run automatically when Windows starts. Click Next.

5. Click Yes, defragment my disk regularly and click Next (see Figure 20.1).

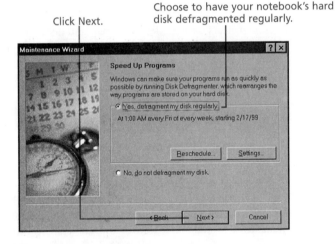

Click Next.

Choose to have your notebook's hard disk defragmented regularly.

FIGURE 20.1 You can choose which maintenance utilities you want Maintenance Wizard to run.

Configure the Utilities To configure the maintenance utilities, click the Reschedule or Settings button and enter your preferences. The Reschedule button lets you set the time at which Windows runs the utility. The Settings button enables you to enter preferences for how the utility performs its job.

6. Click Yes, scan my hard disk for errors regularly and click Next.

7. Click Yes, delete unnecessary files regularly and click Next.

8. Click When I click Finish, perform each scheduled task for the first time (if desired), and click Finish.

Reclaiming Hard Disk Space

As you create and edit files, delete folders and files, install programs, and explore the Internet, Windows and your applications store temporary files in various folders on your hard disk. To reclaim this disk space, you can use Disk Cleanup to find and delete these files.

 Quickly Clean a Disk To quickly run Disk Cleanup, right-click a drive icon in My Computer and choose Properties. Click the Disk Cleanup button.

To clear useless files from your notebook's hard disk, take the following steps:

1. Open the Start menu, point to Programs, Accessories, System Tools, and click Disk Cleanup.

2. Open the Drives drop-down list, click the letter of the drive you want to clean up, and click OK. The Disk Cleanup message box appears briefly as Disk Cleanup determines how much disk space it can clear. Then the Disk Cleanup dialog box appears, prompting you to enter your preferences.

3. Click to place a check mark in the box for each type of file you want Disk Cleanup to remove from the hard disk (see Figure 20.2).

Place a check mark next to each file type you want removed.

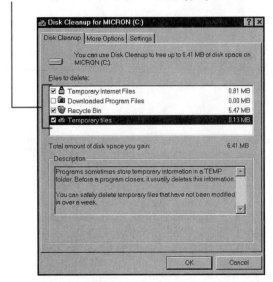

FIGURE 20.2 You can specify which files you want Disk Cleanup to remove.

4. To free additional disk space, click the More Options tab.

5. To remove a program or a Windows component, click one of the Clean Up buttons and follow the instructions.

6. Click the Settings tab.

7. Make sure the If this drive runs low on disk space, automatically run Disk Cleanup check box is selected.

8. Click OK.

Scanning Your Hard Disk for Errors

Any time your notebook shuts down prematurely (without properly shutting down Windows), files and folders can be damaged or your notebook can lose track of temporary files. This can cause your notebook to run more slowly and crash more frequently. To search your hard disk for

corrupted and misplaced files, run ScanDisk every month or so. Take the
following steps:

1. Open the Start menu, point to Programs, Accessories, System
   Tools, and click ScanDisk.

2. Click the letter of the disk you want ScanDisk to check, as
   shown in Figure 20.3.

Select a standard or
thorough disk check.

Choose the disk you
want ScanDisk to check.

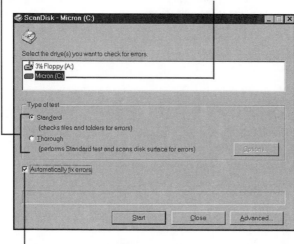

Let ScanDisk automatically fix any problems.

FIGURE 20.3 Enter the desired settings to tell ScanDisk how to
proceed.

3. Choose one of the following options:

   Standard to check files and folders for errors without
   checking the actual surface of the disk.

   Thorough to check files and folders and check the surface
   of the disk to ensure that the storage medium is capable of
   reliably storing data.

A Thorough Check Can Take Hours   If your notebook has a hard disk that's over two gigabytes, a thorough check can take an hour or more.

4. To have ScanDisk proceed without prompting you for confirmation, click Automatically fix errors to place a check in its box.

5. Click the Start button. ScanDisk checks the files and folders on the selected disk, repairs any damaged files or folders, and displays the ScanDisk Results dialog box indicating what ScanDisk has done.

6. Click the Close button.

Defragmenting Your Hard Disk

As you save and delete files, your files become *fragmented*. That is, parts of each file are stored on areas of the disk that are located far away from other storage areas. This slows down your disk and makes it more likely that files will be lost or damaged. Disk Defragmenter rewrites the files, placing the parts of each file on neighboring storage areas. To run Disk Defragmenter, take the following steps:

1. Choose Start, Programs, Accessories, System Tools, Disk Defragmenter.

2. Open the drop-down list and choose the letter of the disk you want to defragment (see Figure 20.4).

3. Click OK.

4. If desired, click Show Details to see Defragmenter in action.

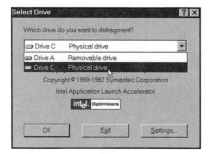

FIGURE 20.4 Choose the letter of the disk you want to defragment.

Optimizing Your Program Files Defragmenter can also place program files at the beginning of your disk so that they run faster. Click the Settings button to enter your preferences. Make sure Rearrange program files so my programs will start faster is checked.

Updating Windows

Microsoft continues to perfect Windows 98, adding new device drivers and improving its performance. To ensure that you have the latest version of Windows, you should check for and install updates on a regular basis. Windows Update can automatically download and install updates from Microsoft's Web site.

Have You Registered? To use Windows Update, you must have a registered copy of Windows 98. The first time you run Windows Update, it prompts you to register Windows.

To run Windows Update, take the following steps:

1. Choose Start, Windows Update.

2. Internet Explorer runs and connects you to the Windows Update page. If you are prompted to register, click Yes and proceed with step 3; otherwise, skip to step 5.

3. When the Registration wizard appears, click Next.

4. Follow the onscreen instructions and complete the forms to register your copy of Windows 98.

5. Click the Product Updates link or its equivalent. The Security Warning dialog box appears asking if you want to install and run Microsoft Windows Update Active Setup.

6. Click Yes. Internet Explorer downloads, installs, and runs Active Setup. Active Setup displays a dialog box asking if you want it to check for installed Components.

7. Click Yes. Active Setup displays a list of components and updates that are available for downloading.

8. Click the check box next to each component and update you want to download (see Figure 20.5).

9. Click the Download button in the upper-right corner of the window. Windows Update copies the selected components to your notebook and installs them. You might need to restart your notebook.

Click Download.

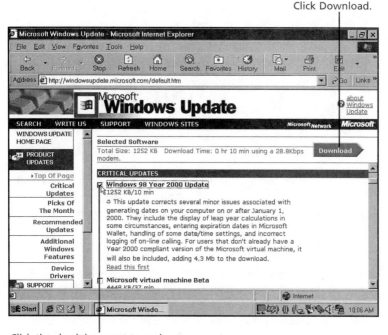

Click the check box next to each component
and update you want to install.

FIGURE 20.5 Active Setup displays a list of additional components
and updates you can download and install.

This lesson showed you how to keep your notebook in tip-top shape. In
the next lesson, you learn how to improve your notebook's performance
with Windows utilities.

LESSON 21
Souping Up Your Notebook

This lesson shows you how to optimize your notebook's performance.

Although the latest breed of notebooks is nearly as powerful as its desktop counterparts, your notebook might not perform as well as you would like. It might start slowly, take a little too long to load files, or appear a bit sluggish when performing some tasks.

Of course, you can improve your notebook's overall performance by installing more memory or a faster hard drive, but upgrading a notebook is no easy (or cheap) task. Fortunately, you can optimize your system without purchasing expensive upgrades. This lesson reveals some relatively easy adjustments that will help your notebook achieve its full potential.

Speeding Up the Hard Drive

Compared to RAM (memory), your hard disk is slow. To increase the speed at which Windows reads from the disk, you can increase the amount of RAM used for the *read-ahead buffer*. This enables your system to read more than what is immediately needed from the disk and store it in RAM, where Windows can quickly access it.

 Read-Ahead Buffer A *read-ahead buffer* is a temporary storage area in a computer's memory that helps the computer access data more quickly. The computer reads more data from the disk than is currently needed and stores it in the buffer where the processor can quickly access it.

To change the read-ahead buffer setting for your notebook's hard drive, take the following steps:

1. Right-click My Computer and choose Properties or Alt+click My Computer.

2. Click the Performance tab.

3. Click the File System button.

4. Open the Typical role of this computer drop-down list and choose Mobile or docking system (see Figure 21.1).

5. Drag the Read-ahead optimization slider to specify the amount of RAM to use for the read-ahead buffer. For full optimization, make sure the slider is all the way to the right.

6. Click OK.

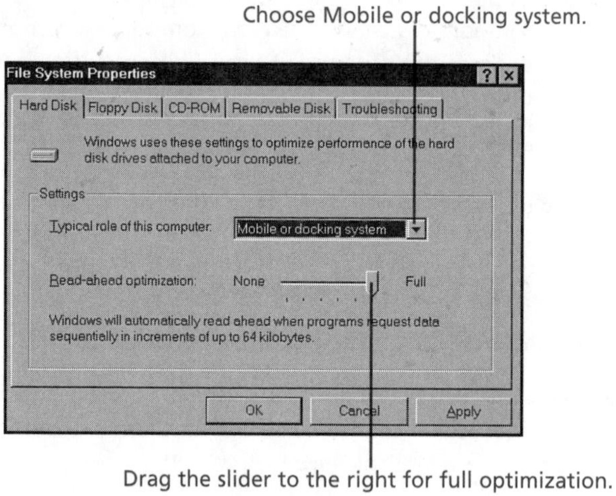

Choose Mobile or docking system.

Drag the slider to the right for full optimization.

FIGURE 21.1 Increase the read-ahead buffer to optimize your notebook's hard drive performance.

Less Than 16MB RAM? If your system has less than 16MB of RAM, you might want to *decrease* the amount of RAM used for the read-ahead buffer one or two notches to reserve more memory for Windows and your applications.

Speeding Up the CD-ROM Drive

Even a fast CD-ROM drive is slower than RAM (memory) or your hard disk drive. To speed it up, you can have Windows read more of the CD than is immediately needed and store the data in RAM, where it is easily accessible.

 Supplemental Cache *Cache* (pronounced "cash") is a temporary storage area in a computer's memory that enables the processor to quickly access data and program instructions.

To change the cache size for your CD-ROM drive, take the following steps:

1. Right-click My Computer and choose Properties.

2. On the Performance tab, click the File System button.

3. On the CD-ROM tab, open the Optimize access pattern for drop-down list and choose the speed of your CD-ROM drive or the highest speed available (see Figure 21.2).

4. Drag the Supplemental cache size slider to specify the amount of RAM to use. Click OK.

Drag the slider to the left to decrease the
cache size or to the right to increase it.

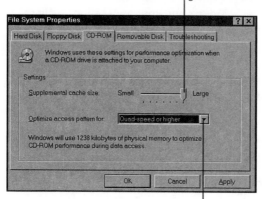

Choose the speed that matches that of your CD-ROM drive.

FIGURE 21.2 If you use your CD-ROM drive frequently, crank up
the supplemental cache size.

**Decrease the Setting When CD-ROM Player Is Not in
Use** If you rarely use your CD-ROM drive and your
system has less than 32MB of RAM, decrease the
supplemental cache size to give Windows and your
applications more memory.

Adjusting the Virtual Memory Settings

Windows and your applications typically require more RAM (memory)
than is installed on your computer. To make up for any memory shortfall,
Windows uses your hard disk drive as *virtual memory*. For optimum performance, make sure Windows is set up to manage virtual memory. If
your notebook has two or more hard drives, you should enter settings to
tell Windows to use the fastest drive with the most free space.

Clear Useless Files from Your Hard Disk   To ensure that Windows and your applications have the memory they need to function properly, your hard drive should have at least 30MB of free space to use as virtual memory. If your hard drive has less than 30MB of free space, use Disk Cleanup to remove useless files and remove any programs you no longer use.

To check and/or adjust the virtual memory settings, take the following steps:

1. Right-click My Computer and choose Properties or Alt+click My Computer.

2. Click the Performance tab.

3. Click the Virtual Memory button.

4. If your notebook has only one hard drive or the fastest hard drive with the most free space is already being used for virtual memory, click Let Windows manage my virtual memory settings, click OK, and you're done. If your notebook has two or more hard drives and you want to change the drive that Windows uses for virtual memory, choose Let me specify my own virtual memory settings and proceed to step 5 (see Figure 21.3).

5. Open the Hard Disk drop-down list and choose the letter of the fastest drive that has the most free space.

6. Click OK.

7. When prompted to confirm, click Yes.

8. Click the Virtual Memory button.

9. Click Let Windows manage my virtual memory settings and click OK.

Choose the fastest hard drive with the most space.

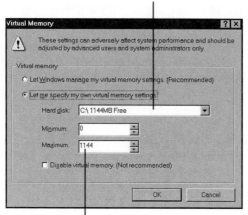

Enter the total amount of free space on the drive.

FIGURE 21.3 Enter your preferences to tell Windows how to manage virtual memory.

Optimizing Your Modem

When you're browsing the Web or using a commercial online service, your modem limits your cruising speed. To ensure that your modem is communicating at top speed, make sure the correct modem driver is loaded and check your modem settings:

1. Open the Start menu, point to Settings, and click Control Panel.

2. Double-click the Modems icon.

3. Make sure the modem list displays the name of your modem (see Figure 21.4).

Wrong Modem Driver? If the wrong modem driver is installed, the modem might not be transferring data at optimum speeds. For example, if your notebook has a 56Kbps modem but a 28.8Kbps driver is installed, the modem will transfer data at 28.8Kbps—half the speed at which it is capable of transferring data.

4. If your modem is not in the list, click the Add button and follow the onscreen instructions to install the driver for your modem. (You can install modem drivers from the Windows CD or from the disk that came with your modem; in most cases, it is best to use the driver that came with your modem.)

Select the old driver and click Remove.

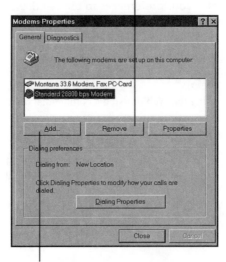

Click the Add button to install a new modem driver.

FIGURE 21.4 Make sure the correct modem driver is installed for your modem.

5. If you installed a new driver, click the name of the old driver and click the Remove button.

6. Click the Properties button.

7. Open the Maximum Speed drop-down list and choose 115200.
   Even if this speed is beyond the speed your modem supports,
   choose the maximum setting. Your modem will make the necessary adjustment.

8. Click OK to return to the Modems Properties dialog box.

9. Click Close to save your changes.

Streamlining the Windows Startup

When you install a program, it might set itself up to run automatically on
startup. In some cases, you might want the program to run when Windows
starts; for example, to protect your notebook against viruses, an anti-virus
program might run every time you start your notebook. In addition, if you
always use a particular program, you can have Windows load the program
to save you the time of selecting it from the Start menu.

However, when programs run on startup, Windows takes more time to
load. To make Windows start faster, take the following steps to prevent
any programs you don't use from running automatically:

1. Right-click a blank area of the Windows taskbar and click
   Properties.

2. Click the Start Menu Programs tab.

3. Click the Remove button.

4. If the Programs icon has a plus sign next to it, click the plus sign
   to display the contents of the Programs folder.

5. Click the plus sign next to the StartUp icon.

6. Click the name of the program you do not want Windows to run
   at startup, as shown in Figure 21.5.

7. Click the Remove button.

8. Repeat steps 6 and 7 to prevent Windows from running any other
   programs at startup.

9. Click the Close button.

Click the name of the program.

Remove Shortcuts/Folders   ? X

To remove an item from the Start menu, select the item and click
Remove.

- Programs
  - Accessories
  - Internet Explorer
  - Lotus Applications
  - Microsoft Data Access Components 1.5
  - Office Tools
  - Online Services
  - PaperPort
  - StartUp
    - Microsoft Office
    - outlook
    - Smartctr
  - TravRoute Door-to-Door CoPilot
  - TurboTax Deluxe 1998

    [Remove]   [Close]

Click Remove.

FIGURE 21.5   To prevent Windows from running a program on
startup, remove the program from the StartUp folder.

Shave Seconds Off Windows Startup   If the Windows
desktop is set up to display Active Components or
other Web content, you can make Windows start
faster by turning off Web content. Right-click a blank
area of the desktop, point to Active Desktop, and click
View As Web Page to remove the check mark. To save
more time, remove any shortcuts on the desktop that
you don't use.

This lesson showed you how to optimize your notebook's performance. In
the next lesson, you learn how to configure your notebook's system settings to enhance its performance.

LESSON 22

Checking Your Notebook's BIOS Settings

This lesson shows you how to configure your notebook's system settings to control its operation and enhance its performance.

Your computer's BIOS (basic input/output system) acts as a control center for your notebook's components. The BIOS settings tell your notebook the date and time, the type of floppy and hard disk drives it has, where to look for startup instructions, whether your notebook has a Plug and Play BIOS, when to power down devices to save power, and how to communicate with the various ports.

Because the BIOS is in control of your notebook, it's not something you should play around with. Changing the hard drive settings can bring your notebook to its knees, preventing it from accessing anything on the hard disk. That doesn't mean you should avoid checking out your notebook's BIOS settings, however. You can learn a great deal about your notebook by looking at the BIOS settings without changing them. In addition, you can enhance your notebook's performance with a few simple tweaks. This lesson shows you how to safely check your notebook's BIOS settings, make some safe changes, and avoid mistakes.

 Keep a Log Keep a *written* log of any BIOS setting you change and the change you made so that you can change it back if you encounter problems. Do not change any settings you don't understand.

Accessing the BIOS Setup Screen

To access the BIOS setup screen, you must press a special key or key combination after you turn on your notebook but before Windows starts. Your notebook's documentation should specify the key or key combination you must press. If the documentation isn't handy, watch the screen carefully during startup; it typically displays the key you must press to enter the setup program. Take the following steps to access the BIOS setup screen:

1. Turn on your notebook and press the specified key or key combination. The BIOS Setup screen appears, as shown in Figure 22.1. Your screen might differ depending on the BIOS and its version number.

 Typical Keystrokes for Accessing System Setup
Most systems use the same standard keystrokes for calling up the setup screen: F1, F2, F3, or Delete.

2. Press the left or right arrow key to change from one menu of options to another.

3. Use the down and up arrow keys to highlight an option you want to check or change.

4. To change a setting, take one of the following steps:

   Press the plus or minus key to change a value displayed in brackets, for instance to change [Off] to [On].

   Highlight an option preceded by an arrow and press Enter to view its submenu.

   Highlight the setting and press Enter to display a pop-up menu with available options. Highlight the desired option and press Enter.

Highlight an option and press [+] or [-] to change the setting.

```
         PhoenixBIOS Setup – Copyright 1985-95 Phoenix Technologies Ltd.
   Main      Advanced    Security    Power      Boot        Exit


  System Time:            [15:25:47]                      Item Specific Help
  System Date:            [09/03/1999]
  Diskette A:             [1.44 MB, 3½"]
▶ IDE Adapter 0 Master (C: 2161 Mb)               <Tab>, <Shift-Tab>, or
▶ IDE Adapter 1 Master (CD-ROM)                   <Enter> selects field.
  Video Display Device:   [CRT & LCD]
  External Cache          [Enabled]
▶ Boot Options
▶ Numlock                 [Off]

  System Memory:            640 KB
  Extended Memory:           23 MB


      Help     ↑↓    Select Item    /+    Change Values    F9    Setup Defaults
      Exit     ←→    Select Menu   Enter  Select ▶ Sub-Menu F10  Previous Values
```

Highlight an option and press Enter to view its submenu.

FIGURE 22.1   The BIOS setup screen consists of several menus packed with system settings.

No Mouse Control   Because the BIOS setup runs before your computer runs the mouse driver, you must use your keyboard to navigate the BIOS Setup screen and enter your changes. This can be a little tricky if you're not accustomed to it.

Bypassing the Floppy Drive on Startup

If your notebook has a built-in floppy drive, chances are that your notebook is set up to first look to the floppy disk drive for boot instructions on startup. You can reduce the time it takes your system to start by having your notebook look to the hard drive first. With the BIOS setup screen displayed, take the following steps:

1. Press the right arrow key to highlight the Boot menu.

2. Press the down arrow key to highlight Hard Drive.

3. Press the plus key to move this option to the top of the list (see Figure 22.2).

4. Press the left or right arrow key to highlight the Main menu.

5. Press the down arrow key to highlight Boot Options and press Enter.

6. Press the down arrow key to highlight Floppy Check [Enabled] and press the plus key to change the setting to [Disabled].

7. Press the Esc key to return to the Main menu.

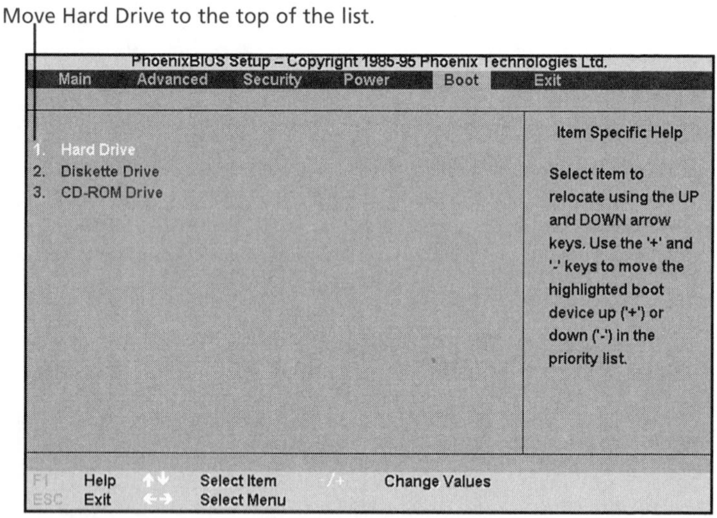

Move Hard Drive to the top of the list.

FIGURE 22.2 You can shave several seconds off the time it takes your notebook to boot by telling it to look to the hard drive first.

Checking the Parallel Port Setting

Most newer printers and other peripherals that connect to the parallel port support bi-directional communication, which enables the peripheral to communicate with your notebook. However, your notebook's parallel port must support bi-directional communications and the parallel port option in the BIOS must be set to bi-directional mode.

 A Bi-Directional Printer Needs a Bi-Directional Cable   Make sure you connect your bi-directional printer to your system unit's printer port with a bi-directional printer cable (also called an IEEE 1284 cable).

To check and/or change the setting for your notebook's parallel port, take the following steps:

1. Press the right or left arrow key to highlight the Advanced menu.

2. Press the down arrow key to highlight Integrated Peripherals and press Enter.

3. Press the down arrow key to highlight the Parallel Mode option, as shown in Figure 22.3.

4. Take one of the following steps:

    Press the plus or minus key to change the setting to [Bi-Directional] or [ECP] (Extended Capabilities Port).

    Press Enter to display the pop-up menu, use the up or down arrow key to highlight Bi-Directional or ECP (Extended Capabilities Port), and press Enter.

5. Press the Esc key to return to the Advanced menu.

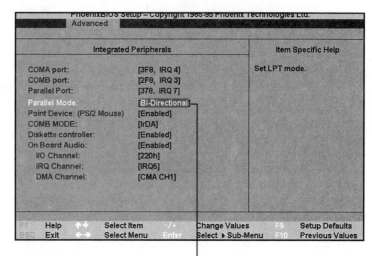

Highlight the option and press the [+] or [-] key to change the setting to Bi-Directional or ECP.

FIGURE 22.3   To use the advanced capabilities of your notebook's parallel port, choose Bi-Directional mode.

Checking Your Notebook's Power-Saving Settings

Although Windows comes with a power-management utility, your computer might have built-in power conservation features. These features can conflict with Windows power management settings or with other software. You can adjust or disable these settings in the BIOS Setup. Take the following steps to check and/or change the power-saving settings:

1. Press the left or right arrow key to highlight the Power menu.

2. Use the down arrow key to highlight the Power Savings option (see Figure 22.4).

3. Take one of the following steps:

    Press the plus key to cycle through the available options. (To disable the power-saving features, choose [Off].)

Press Enter to display the pop-up menu, use the down
arrow key to highlight the desired option, and press Enter.

4. If you chose [Customize] in step 3, enter the desired settings for
powering down the display and hard disk.

To enter your own preferences, choose Customize.

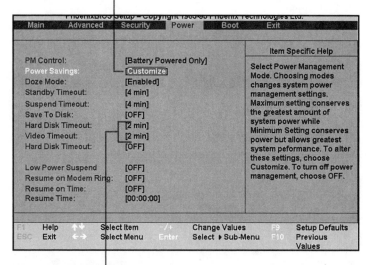

With Customize selected, you can enter individual timeout settings for the
hard drive and monitor.

FIGURE 22.4   You can choose a standard set of power-saving settings or enter custom settings.

Saving Your Changes

As you change BIOS settings, the settings are recorded but not entered.
You must save the settings and exit. After you exit, Windows starts.

Exit Without Saving Changes   If you change a setting by mistake or are not sure if you made changes,
choose the option for exiting *without* saving changes.

To exit system setup and save the changes you entered, take the following steps:

1. Press the left or right arrow key to highlight the Exit menu.

2. Press the down arrow key to highlight Save Changes & Exit (see Figure 22.5).

3. Press Enter.

Highlight the Exit menu.

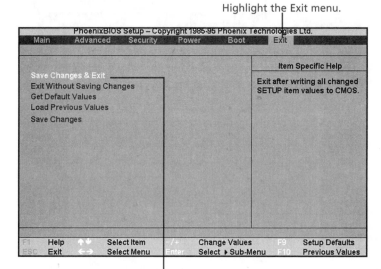

Highlight Save Changes & Exit.

FIGURE 22.5 When you're done entering changes, save the changes and exit the system setup.

This lesson showed you how to configure your notebook's system settings to improve its performance and control the way it operates. In the next lesson, you learn how to deter someone from stealing your notebook.

LESSON 23

Securing Your Notebook: Anti-Theft Guide

This lesson shows you how to deter notebook theft and help you recover your notebook from theft or loss.

Though small and easy to tote around, your notebook probably cost you as much as a good used car. And the programs and data you have stored on your notebook might be even more valuable. To protect your investment, spend a little time and effort to protect it from theft or loss. This lesson shows you just what to do.

Taking Basic, Inexpensive Security Steps

You can spend hundreds of dollars on anti-theft devices, as you'll see in the next section. However, the best security steps you can take cost next to nothing. To secure your notebook, and help you recover it later, take the following steps:

- Write down the serial number of your notebook. It should be molded into the case or written on a sticker attached to the notebook. If your notebook is lost or stolen, you'll need the serial number to file a police report and complete the required insurance forms.

- Take a picture of your notebook and store the picture with your sales receipt.

- If you personally own the notebook (it's not the property of the company you work for), contact your insurance company to determine whether the notebook is covered. Most homeowner's policies do not cover equipment used for business. You might need to pay a little extra on your insurance premium to add coverage.

- Use an engraving tool or permanent pen to write your name, address, and telephone number on your notebook. If you lose your notebook and some honest soul finds it, the person will need to know how to contact you.

- Stick a business card in your carrying case and tape a business card to any peripheral devices, including your battery, external disk drives, and portable printer.

- Camouflage your notebook. Use a carrying case that doesn't look like a notebook carrying case. This makes it tougher for thieves to identify the contents of the case as a valuable notebook. Check out www.spireusa.com for notebook carrying cases that don't look like notebook carrying cases.

- Back up the data files stored on your notebook. Ideally, you should back up everything because your programs and Internet software have configuration settings that you might have trouble reproducing. However, data files are most important.

- When you use the restroom at the airport, don't hang your notebook carrying case on the hooks near the entrance. Keep your notebook on your shoulder or carry it into the stall with you. If you take the notebook in the stall with you, don't set it on the ground because someone can reach under the partition and grab it. Hang it on a hook or at least wrap the strap around your foot.

- Never leave your notebook in your car, especially on the front seat. If you must leave your notebook in the car, and temperature permits, place it in the trunk.

- Keep an eye on your notebook when you're passing through airport security, checking into your motel room, renting a car, and at other places where you tend to shift your focus from your notebook.

Checking Out Anti-Theft Gear

Although common sense measures are the best way to protect your note-book from theft, you can purchase special anti-theft devices, including notebook locks and alarms, to further protect your notebook when you can't be there to watch it. The following list describes some of the more popular anti-theft devices on the market:

- **Kensington MicroSaver Security System**   The MicroSaver Security System consists of a lock that attaches to your note-book's security slot and a cable that you wrap around a station-ary object. Removing the lock from the security slot requires a key; without the key, a thief would have to damage the note-book, making it tough to sell (see Figure 23.1). To learn more about Kensington computer security products, go to www.kensington.com.

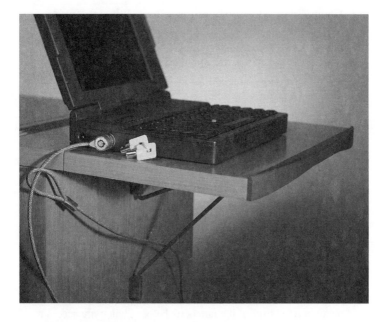

FIGURE 23.1   Most notebook locks attach to the notebook's secu-rity slot. (Photo courtesy of Kensington.)

- **DEFCON 1 alarm/lock**   The DEFCON 1 from Targus (www.targus.com) is an alarm and lock combination. The alarm is motion sensitive, so if someone tries to move the notebook, the movement activates the alarm. The alarm also sounds if someone tries to cut the cable. The DEFCON 1 comes with an adapter for connecting it to your notebook's security slot. If your notebook does not have a security slot, you attach the device to your carrying case. DEFCON 3 is a carrying case with a built-in alarm.

- **Notebook Guardian**   The Notebook Guardian from PC Guardian (www.pcguardian.com) is similar to the Kensington MicroSaver in that it attaches to your notebook's security slot. If your notebook doesn't have a security slot, PC Guardian offers a lock that attaches to a fixed floppy drive. Or, you can purchase a mounting adapter that attaches to your notebook with a special adhesive.

- **CompuTrace**   CompuTrace is a software utility that works along with your modem to help catch the criminal (or the person who purchased your notebook from the criminal). At regular intervals, CompuTrace silently dials into a database system and submits the phone number from which the call was placed along with information identifying your notebook. If your notebook is stolen, report the theft to CompuTrace and the service starts monitoring the system for a call from your notebook. At the time this book was written, the product was selling for $89.95, which included one year of service. For details, visit www.computrace.com.

- **Kensington FloppyLock**   FloppyLock hooks onto your floppy disk drive to prevent someone from inserting a disk without your permission. This secures your data by preventing someone from copying sensitive material from your notebook. It also prevents someone from loading a disk that contains a virus.

- **Biometric ID systems**   A biometric ID system identifies you as an authorized user of the notebook before giving you access to it. Biometric systems use fingerprint, voice, or face recognition rather than a password to identify you. There are several such systems on the market, including American Biometric's

BioMouse, a fingerprint recognition device that attaches to
the parallel port (visit www.abio.com) and QVoice's Star Trek
Biometric Security System, a facial and voice recognition
system that requires a video camera and audio input (visit
www.qvtrek.com).

- **ThinkPad Asset ID**   Newer IBM ThinkPads support a new
  security system that prevents notebooks from "walking out" of
  companies. The device operates like anti-theft tags used in
  department stores. An antenna connected to the notebook
  transmits data to a receiver, which then sends data back to the
  notebook to turn on password protection. For details, visit
  www.ibm.com.

No Security Slot?   Examine your notebook carefully
to find the security slot—it's pretty small, but most
notebooks from the top manufacturers have a built-in
slot. If your notebook does not have a security slot,
purchase a universal lock. The lock typically comes
with a metal plate that you glue to your notebook
case.

Disable Alarm at the Airport   If you use an alarm for
security, be sure to disable it whenever you are moving your notebook at the airport. You don't
want the alarm to sound when you're going through
security.

Checking Out Security/Encryption Software

Although hardware security devices are best for preventing outright theft,
software security solutions are better at preventing sensitive data from
falling into the wrong hands. In addition, security software can render
your notebook useless to the average criminal. Read through the following
list to learn about the most popular security software on the market:

- **SecureWin**   SecureWin by Cipher Logics enables you to
  encrypt all files in a folder with the click of a button. SecureWin
  supports six of the most effective encryption schemes to protect
  your data and programs from unauthorized access. To learn more
  about this product and download a free, 30-day trial version,
  visit www.securewin.com.

- **Norton DiskLock**   Norton DiskLock enables you to password-
  protect your entire system or only sensitive files. The software
  loads before the system software, preventing unauthorized users
  from bypassing the password or booting from a floppy disk.
  DiskLock also includes a screen blanker to protect your notebook when you're not there. For more information about
  DiskLock and Symantec's complete line of security products,
  visit www.symantec.com.

- **DataSAFE**   One of the more interesting security products on
  the market, NOVaSTOR's DataSAFE enables you to drag files
  into a virtual safe and assign it a combination. You can use a
  safe to store your sensitive data files or send the safe securely
  via email to a friend or colleague. As long as the recipient has
  the right combination, he or she can open the safe and retrieve
  the files. For details, visit data-encryption.com/datasheets/
  dsafe.html.

- **LapJack**   One of the more innovative products of the bunch,
  LapJack is a hardware/software combination that prevents unauthorized users from starting your notebook. With LapJack, your
  notebook won't start unless you insert a special key in the parallel port. Without the key, the notebook is useless to anyone who
  takes it. For information about LapJack, visit www.sspusa.com.

- **SecurePC**   RSA's SecurePC is a no-frills encryption program
  for files and email. When you install SecurePC, it places a button in the Windows Explorer toolbar, providing you with one-
  click access to file encryption. For details about RSA, visit
  www.rsa.com. To obtain information about SecurePC and
  download a free, 30-day evaluation copy, visit
  www.securitydynamics.com.

More Security/Encryption Software   This list describes a small sample of security/encryption software on the market. Use your favorite Internet search tool, visit your local computer store, or call your favorite mail-order computer store to locate additional security software.

Recovering a Lost or Stolen Notebook

Even if you take all the precautions in this lesson and use the best security gadgets and software on the market, there's still a chance you might leave your notebook in your motel room or some clever thief will nab it. In the event that your notebook is lost or stolen, don't give up—you might be able to get it back or at least recover a portion of the cost. Take the following steps:

- If you think you left your notebook behind, immediately contact the business, motel, or other establishment where you think you might have left it.

- Contact the police and fill out a police report. If your notebook is recovered and turned over to the police, they need to know how to contact you. Provide a description of the notebook and its serial number. Occasionally, a thief will pawn the notebook; a reputable pawn shop owner will call in the serial number to the police.

- Contact your insurance agent and file a claim. Although insurance companies rarely cover the full cost of computer equipment, they might reimburse you for an amount equal to a notebook with similar capabilities.

- Claim the loss on your next tax return. Although the tax code places strict limits on the amount you can deduct for losses from thefts, it might be enough to cover your insurance deductible.

- If CompuTrace or a similar computer-tracking program is installed on your notebook, call the service to let them know that

your notebook is missing. The service needs you to inform it of
the loss so that it can monitor for incoming calls.

 White Collar Crime   Most notebook theft is the result
of employees or contractors walking out with the
company's equipment.

This lesson showed you how to prevent your notebook from being lost or
stolen and recover your notebook if it is lost or stolen. At the end of this
book are several useful appendixes to help you find accessories and technical support for your notebook.

APPENDIX A

Notebook Toys and Accessories

This appendix opens your eyes to the many notebook add-ons available in the market.

Although your notebook is a self-contained PC, its ports and PC card slots make it easy to upgrade and accessorize. In addition, because your notebook is portable, you might need to use power and phone adapters to make it compatible with the equipment and services available wherever you travel.

Fortunately, hundreds of developers and manufacturers have designed add-ons and accessories for notebooks, ranging from basic devices, such as memory cards and external drives, to specialty items, such as acoustic phone couplers and international power adapters. The following sections introduce you to the most popular notebook toys and accessories on the market, opening your eyes to the possibilities of portable computing.

Notebook Carrying Cases

If your notebook came with its own carrying case, you have probably realized that it's inadequate. It's as though the manufacturer designed it thinking that you would leave your AC adapter, extra battery, and any other peripherals at home. Consider purchasing a more practical, roomier carrying case. Many carrying cases also feature improved theft protection in the form of better locks and built-in alarms. Other cases are designed to look like backpacks or standard luggage to prevent thieves from easily identifying the contents as a notebook.

PORT Incorporated (at www.port.com) offers the best selection of carrying cases, including notebook backpacks, the EasyRoller (shown in Figure A.1), and a wide selection of more standard fare.

FIGURE A.1   PORT Incorporated markets the EasyRoller notebook carrying case. (Photo courtesy of PORT Incorporated.)

PC Card Modems and Network Adapters

By far the most popular add-ons for notebooks are PC card modems and network adapters. If your notebook doesn't come with a built-in modem, the first accessory you should purchase is a PC card modem. This gives you access to the Internet and enables you to connect to your desktop PC or network when you're on the road.

If you work for a company that has a network or would prefer to network your notebook and desktop PC rather than connecting them with a parallel or serial data cable, consider purchasing a PC card network adapter for your notebook. This enables you to quickly plug into a network to access shared files and equipment, such as printers and storage devices.

Find Out What's Available 3Com and Motorola both offer a wide variety of PC card modems and network adapters. Check out 3Com at www.3com.com or visit Motorola at www.motorola.com. Appendix B, "Notebook Suppliers," includes contact information for retailers.

PC Card Memory

Some notebooks skimp on memory and provide no easy way to add memory internally. Many notebook manufacturers require that you send in your notebook to have the memory upgraded in order to preserve the warranty. In such cases, consider adding memory by inserting a PC memory card. See Appendix B for mail-order companies that specialize in notebook accessories.

External Storage Devices

Although your notebook has an internal hard drive and might include a floppy or CD-ROM drive, you might need additional storage. For instance, if you commonly take your presentations on the road, an external Zip drive enables you to store an entire presentation on a removable disk. The following list describes some of the more popular external storage devices for notebooks:

Hard drive Most newer notebooks include a built-in hard drive and an extra drive bay. If your notebook doesn't have an extra drive bay, you might be able to attach an external hard drive to the parallel port or insert it as a PC card. Contact your notebook manufacturer or visit its Web site to determine your options.

Zip drive   If your notebook has an open drive bay, consider purchasing a Zip Notebook drive from Iomega (www.iomega.com). Zip drives enable you to swap 100MB Zip disks, making them perfect for storing presentations or for backing up your system. As of the writing of this book, Zip Notebook drives were available for only Compaq, Toshiba, and IBM notebooks. If your notebook has a USB port, Iomega has a USB Zip drive.

DVD drive   Although most notebooks have a built-in CD-ROM drive, few support DVD. If you want to view DVD movies when you're on a trip or you store presentations on DVD discs, consider purchasing a DVD drive.

 Bullet Drive Express   Road Warrior International has a device called Bullet Drive Express that enables you to connect a standard 2.5-inch EIDE hard drive to your notebook's PC card slot. If you purchase the Bullet Drive case with a larger hard drive, you might be able to install the larger drive in your notebook and install the smaller (old) hard drive in the Bullet Drive case. See Appendix B for information on contacting Road Warrior International.

Phone Line Testers and Adapters

When you travel, especially to a foreign country, you never know what types of phone jacks and services you will encounter. Fortunately, there are numerous products on the market to help you connect your modem under any conditions:

Phone line tester   Many businesses and hotels have digital phone lines that carry a higher level of current than standard analog phone lines found in homes. Although digital phone jacks are identical to analog jacks, plugging your modem into a digital jack can damage your modem. A phone line tester has an LED that indicates whether the jack is safe. 1-800-Batteries carries a digital enabler that enables you to plug your modem safely into any phone jack, analog or digital.

Wireless PC card modem   Although your cell phone can carry your voice over wireless connections, it needs help to carry digital transmissions. A wireless PC card modem plugs into your notebook's PC card slot and connects to a cellular receiver. Check out RIM's (Research in Motion) wireless PC card, shown in Figure A.2, at www.rim.net.

FIGURE A.2   RIM's wireless PC card gives your notebook the power to connect to the Internet without a cable. (Photo courtesy of Research In Motion.)

Acoustic coupler   The best way to connect an analog modem is to plug it into a standard phone jack. If you're on the road and no jack is available, you can use an acoustic coupler to connect the modem to a telephone handset, as shown in Figure A.3.

Retractable phone cord   Another good accessory to have with you on road trips, a retractable phone cord provides the flexibility you need to connect to phone jacks placed in odd locations in a hotel room or office.

Acoustic Coupler with a Cellular Phone? You cannot establish wireless modem communications by connecting a standard PC card (analog) modem to a cellular phone using an acoustic coupler. An analog modem is not equipped to translate signals from a cellular phone.

FIGURE A.3 An acoustic coupler enables you to connect your modem to a standard telephone handset. (Photo courtesy of Road Warrior International.)

 Wireless Connections via GoAmerica If you opt to go cellular with a PC card modem, check out GoAmerica's wireless Internet services at www.goamerica.com. SpeedChoice (www.speedchoice.com) is another popular wireless ISP.

Infrared Adapters and Peripherals

To make use of your notebook's infrared port, you'll have to hunt down the infrared adapters and peripherals you need; they haven't quite made it into the mainstream. However, there are a few products out there worth noting:

Canon BJC-80   You'll find dozens of portable printers on the market, but most require a cable connection to the parallel port. The Canon BJC-80 is one of the few portable printers that supports infrared communications. Check it out at www.ccsi.canon.com. Citizen's Portable PN60 and PN60i also provide full IrDA support.

JetEye infrared adapters   To add infrared capabilities to your desktop PC and printer, check out Extended Systems' wide selection of infrared adapters at www.extendsys.com/products/infrared/. With JetEye adapters, you can add infrared capabilities to any parallel printer, establish wireless network connections, and add infrared support to a desktop PC's serial port.

BayBeamer   BayBeamer is one of the more interesting infrared devices I've seen. You house the device in an open drive bay on your desktop PC and connect it to the IrDA connector (typically not used) on your PC's motherboard. This provides the same communications speeds you get by connecting an infrared device to the serial port, but it places the infrared receiver right at the front of the desktop PC without your having to fiddle with cables. For more information, check out BayBeamer at www.baybeamer.com.

BayBeamer Beware   Before you run out and purchase BayBeamer, make sure your desktop PC's motherboard has an IrDA connector. Check its documentation or contact technical support.

Casio, Kodak, and Sony digital cameras   You can find many digital cameras on the market that support infrared communications, making it easy for you to transfer images from the camera to your notebook. If you're in the market for a digital camera and don't want to mess with cables, make sure the camera has an infrared port.

Personal organizers   Many PDAs (Personal Digital Assistants) support infrared communications, enabling you to quickly connect your PDA to your notebook without the hassle of cables.

USB Adapters and Peripherals

Nearly every new notebook has at least one USB (Universal Serial Bus) port, and each port allows you to connect up to 127 devices, not that you'll find 127 different devices on the market. Here's a brief sampling of the types of devices you will find:

Keyboards   One of the easiest ways to add a full-size keyboard to your notebook is to plug in a USB keyboard. Several companies, including Microsoft and Belkin, have USB keyboards. (You might still need to use the notebook's built-in keyboard for configuring the display's brightness and contrast and for navigating system setup.)

Pointing devices   USB pointing devices are one of the most popular USB add-ons for notebooks. Logitech offers a wide selection of USB pointing devices, including mice, touchpads, and trackballs.

Check Out Logitech for USB Input Devices
Logitech has the widest selection of USB input devices, including keyboards, mice, digital cameras, and game controllers. To check out Logitech's product line, go to www.logitech.com/us/.

Monitors   Although you can attach a standard monitor to your notebook's VGA port, it's much easier to connect it to the USB port, especially if you need to share the monitor between your notebook and desktop PC. Most monitor manufacturers have USB monitors.

Game controllers   Most notebooks don't include a game port. However, you can connect a game controller via the USB port. Check out Microsoft's Sidewinder Precision Pro USB Joystick, Gravis PC Gamepad Pro USB, or (for a total driving experience) Logitech's Wingman Formula Force.

Network adapters   Most notebook users opt to use a PC card to hook up to a network. With a USB network adapter, you can free one of your PC card slots for another device. One of the more interesting USB network adapters on the market is manufactured by LinkSys (www.linksys.com). To network your notebook, you simply connect a USB cable from your network to the adapter and connect a standard RJ-45 network cable from the adapter to the network jack (see Figure A.4).

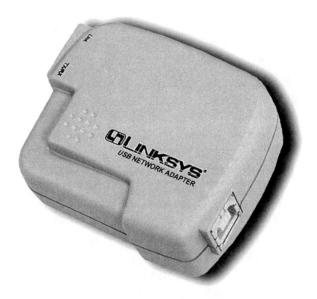

FIGURE A.4   This USB Network Adapter enables you to network your notebook without installing a PC card. (Photo courtesy of LinkSys.)

Modems   Because of the convenience of PC card modems, few users need (or desire) to connect a USB modem to their notebooks. However, if you have a desktop PC that is USB-enabled and uses an external USB modem, you can easily share the modem with your notebook.

Digital cameras   If you're looking for a digital camera to take snapshots and download them to your PC, you might not find many that sport a USB port. However, several small digital cameras typically used for teleconferencing (such as Logitech's popular QuickCam) have built-in USB support.

Printers   USB is an ideal technology for sharing a printer between your desktop PC and notebook. Instead of connecting a Y adapter to the printer, you simply connect your notebook to the printer whenever you need to use it. Many newer printers support USB connections.

Scanners   If you ever tried to daisy-chain a scanner and printer together (and get them to both work reliably), you know how frustrating it can be. With a USB scanner, you simply connect the scanner to your PC and then plug the printer into the scanner (or vice versa). You need not worry about the two devices conflicting.

External storage devices   If you're looking for a way to expand your notebook's storage capacity without disassembling it, consider connecting a USB drive. In addition to the standard fare, Iomega (www.iomega.com) offers a 100MB USB Zip drive. Imation (www.imation.com) manufactures a 120MB SuperDisk drive that can handle standard floppy disks, as well, but during the writing of this book, it was available only for the iMac.

Hubs   Hubs act as connecting stations for USB devices. For example, you can plug a 4-port USB hub into your notebook's USB port and connect four USB devices to the hub. Many USB devices, such as printers, act as hubs, thereby providing additional ports. If you purchase a separate hub, look for a self-powered hub. A bus-powered hub quickly drains your notebook's battery.

Adapters   If your notebook or the peripherals you want to connect to your notebook are not USB enabled, you can purchase adapters to add USB capability. Belkin (www.belkin.com) and ADS (www.adstech.com) offer USB PCI cards for desktop PCs. You can connect a standard printer to your notebook's USB port using a special cable; check out Cables to Go at www.cablestogo.com.

External Battery Chargers

If you frequently run your notebook on battery power, it's a good idea to purchase two batteries and charge one while you're using the other. You can do this with an external battery charger, just like those used for camcorders. Just make sure that you purchase a charger that's compatible with the batteries your notebook uses. Check with the manufacturer or ask the retailer to help you choose the right charger.

Power Adapters for Airplanes and Cars

Airplanes and cars don't offer the modern conveniences of your home or office, especially when it comes to power outlets. To keep your notebook running when you're on the road, consider purchasing an emPower adapter or power inverter. These devices plug into the cigarette lighter socket on a car or an emPower socket on an airplane.

StatPower's NotePower 75   NotePower 75 is a device that plugs into any 12-volt DC source, such as a cigarette lighter socket, and provides an outlet for plugging in an AC adapter. You can use NotePower 75 to safely supply power to your notebook, camcorder, or other electronic devices when you're on the road. Check it out at www.statpower.com.

Solar-Powered Notebook?   If you work outside, check out the Mercury II Solar System for portable computers. It comes complete with the solar panels and adapter you need to power your notebook with solar energy. For more information, check out wildwestweb.com/public/Mercury.html.

Power Adapters for International Travel

Without a safe, reliable power source, you won't be doing much work with your notebook on the road. To prepare for travel abroad, make sure you have the power and outlet adapters you need. Several companies offer adapters designed for specific notebooks and countries. Check out www.1800batteries.com for a wide selection of international adapters.

In addition, PORT offers a universal adapter for IBM, Compaq, and Toshiba notebooks. This universal adapter comes with plugs for the U.S., Canada, and Japan; you can purchase plugs for additional countries from PORT.

This appendix listed the most innovative and useful notebook toys and accessories. The next appendix lists mail-order companies that offer the widest selection of notebook toys and accessories.

APPENDIX B

Notebook Suppliers

This appendix points you to the best mail-order retail stores for finding batteries, power supplies, adapters, and other notebook accessories and toys.

In Lesson 11, "Traveling with Your Notebook: Pre-Flight Checklist," you learned that your notebook might require additional accessories on the road. Finding the required accessories can be an exercise in frustration; your local computer store probably doesn't carry a robust supply of notebook accessories.

Your best choice is to track down a mail-order company that specializes in notebook accessories. This appendix lists contact information for the most popular and well-stocked mail-order companies.

 Find the Lowest Mail-Order Prices   If you know a specific product you want to purchase, go to www.wheretobuy.com on the Web and search for the product. wheretobuy.com provides a long list of mail-order companies that carry the product complete with prices and ordering information.

1-800-Batteries

1-800-Batteries offers the best selection of notebook accessories at the lowest prices around. Its Web site provides the search tools you need to locate batteries, adapters, and other accessories that are designed to work with your notebook. You'll also find plenty of useful accessories, such as GPS devices, docking stations, notebook luggage, and travel kits.

Web Site: www.1800batteries.com

Phone: 1-800-746-6140

Road Warrior International

Road Warrior provides both standard and specialty devices for notebooks, including acoustic couplers, phone line testers and conditioners, power adapters for foreign countries, batteries, and PC card memory. The Road Warrior Web site is a great place to browse, even if you're not sure what you need.

Web Site: www.warrior.com

Phone: 1-800-274-4277

LaptopProducts.com

This is a great place to browse popular categories of notebook accessories, adapters, carrying cases, and add-ons. LaptopProducts.com offers a wide selection of products from several of the top manufacturers of notebook equipment.

Web Site: www.traveladapters.com

Phone: 1-888-531-9327

PORT Incorporated

PORT carries a wide selection of notebook accessories, including notebook carrying cases, emPower adapters, digital phone line adapters, and foreign travel kits, along with special devices for specific models.

Web Site: www.port.com

Phone: 1-800-242-3133

TeleAdapt Inc.

If you're a world traveler, TeleAdapt is the place to go for all your international communications needs. TeleAdapt provides a wide selection of modem and power adapters for international travel. Even if you don't need any adapters, TeleAdapt's Help Desk provides important tips and troubleshooting information for travelers.

> Web Site: www.teleadapt.com (for links to the Traveler Help Desk and other useful travel information) or www.teleadaptusa.com (for ordering products)

> Phone: 1-877-835-3232

Konexx

For communications accessories, Konexx can't be beat. Konexx deals in specialty products, such as acoustic couplers (to hook a modem to a standard phone handset), digital phone line adapters (for safely connecting your modem to a digital line), and anti-theft devices.

> Web Site: www.konexx.com

> Phone: 1-800-275-6354

Mobile Planet Inc.

Mobile Planet sells both notebooks and accessories, including batteries and power adapters. Although the Web site can be difficult to connect to, it's worth a visit.

> Web Site: www.mplanet.com

> Phone: 1-800-675-2638

Targus

Targus offers a wide selection of carrying cases, security devices, and phone and power adapters for notebooks. Before you head out on an important business trip, stop at the Targus Web site or call its product hotline to determine what you need and where to get it. The Targus Web site also features some valuable travel tips.

Web Site: www.targus.com

Phone: 1-800-998-8020

PC Connection

PC Connection offers a wide selection of products for both desktop and notebook PCs, so you'll have to do some searching to find the accessory you need. This is a great place to find cables, batteries, power adapters, GPS devices, infrared peripherals and adapters, and much, much more. Because PC Connection is so popular, you can expect some of the lowest prices and most reliable delivery.

Web Site: www.pcconnection.com

Phone: 1-800-800-0009

PC Zone Internet SuperStore

PC Zone is very similar to PC Connection in that it features both desktop and notebook PC products. At the PC Zone Web site, you'll also find links for the PC Zone's partner stores: Toshiba, IBM, Hewlett Packard, Compaq, and 3COM (an excellent place to look for PC card modems and networking accessories).

Web Site: www.pczone.com

Phone: 1-800-408-9663

Pacific Data Solutions (Compaq Accessories)

For a complete selection of Compaq notebook accessories, check out Pacific Data Solutions. Here, you will find the batteries and adapters you need for your Compaq notebook along with PC card USB adapters, power supplies and emPower adapters, cellular cards, and much more.

Web Site: www.pdsweb.com

Phone: 760-806-8088

This appendix listed the mail-order companies that offer the widest selection of notebook toys and accessories. The next appendix provides the contact information you need to get technical support for the most popular notebook brands.

APPENDIX C

Notebook Tech Support Contact Information

This appendix lists technical support Web addresses and phone numbers for the most popular notebook brands.

As you're plugging in PC cards, connecting peripherals, and configuring your notebook, you might run into problems that you can't solve on your own. When you need help, call technical support or connect to your notebook manufacturer's Web site for instructions and troubleshooting tips. Table C.1 lists the most popular notebook manufacturers along with their Web site addresses and technical support numbers.

TABLE C.1 TECHNICAL SUPPORT CONTACT NUMBERS AND WEB SITES

COMPANY	PHONE NUMBER	WEB SITE
Acer	1-800-816-2237	www.acer.com
Compaq	1-800-652-6672	www.compaq.com/support/portables
Dell	1-888-560-8324	support.dell.com/support
Fujitsu	1-800-838-5487	www.fujitsu-pc.com
Gateway	1-800-846-2302	www.gw2k.com/support
Hewlett-Packard	1-970-346-8682	www.hp.com
Hitachi	1-800-448-2244	www.hitachipc.com

COMPANY	PHONE NUMBER	WEB SITE
IBM	1-800-772-2222	www.pc.ibm.com/support
Micron	1-888-349-6972	support.micronpc.com
NEC	1-800-632-4525	support.neccsdeast.com
Panasonic	1-800-527-8675	www.panasonic.com/host/support
Sharp	1-800-237-4277	www.sharp-usa.com
Sony	1-888-476-6972	www.ita.sel.sony.com/support/pc/
Toshiba	1-800-999-4273	www.csd.toshiba.com

 What About Microsoft? Because your notebook's operating system commonly causes problems, you should know how to contact its manufacturer. For help with Windows-related problems, check out Microsoft's Web site at www.microsoft.com and click the Support link or call (425) 635-7222. You are allowed 90 days of free support via phone from the first contact with a Microsoft technical support representative (of course, you must pay long-distance charges for the call).

This appendix provided the contact information you need to get technical support for the most popular notebook brands. If your brand is not covered here, use your favorite Web search tool to find the manufacturer's Web site.

INDEX

D

J-K

L

W

X-Y-Z

Notes

Use this area to record vital information such as important phone
numbers and BIOS settings.

Notes

Use this area to record vital information such as important phone
numbers and BIOS settings.

Notes

Use this area to record vital information such as important phone
numbers and BIOS settings.

Notes

Use this area to record vital information such as important phone numbers and BIOS settings.

Notes

Use this area to record vital information such as important phone numbers and BIOS settings.

Notes

Use this area to record vital information such as important phone
numbers and BIOS settings.

Notes

Use this area to record vital information such as important phone numbers and BIOS settings.

Notes

Use this area to record vital information such as important phone
numbers and BIOS settings.

Enterprise Harmony—Synchronization Software
Mail-In Manufacturer Rebate

$10.⁰⁰ (U.S.)
REBATE
on Extended Systems
Enterprise Harmony—
Synchronization Software

Purchase Enterprise Harmony Synchronization Software and receive $10.00. Enterprise Harmony allows you to synchronize your e-mail, contacts, calendar and tasks with your mobile device and a desktop PC.

See other side for details.

--✂

JetEye *PC* and JetEye *Printer*
Mail-In Manufacturer Rebate

$10.⁰⁰ (U.S.)
REBATE
on Extended Systems
JetEye *PC* and JetEye *Printer*

Purchase Extended Systems JetEye *PC* and/or JetEye *Printer* and receive $10.00. With JetEye and the infrared port built into your handheld PC, camera, and other mobile devices, you will be able to connect to your network, printer or desktop PC within seconds.

See other side for details.

--✂

www.extendedsystems.com
800-235-7576

Enterprise Harmony—Synchronization Software
Mail-In Manufacturer Rebate

This Extended Systems Manufacturer Rebate is offered to the End User customer who has purchased Enterprise Harmony software between June 1, 1999 and December 31, 2000. This coupon entitles the End User to receive a check in the amount of $10.00 (U.S.) for each Enterprise Harmony software purchased, limit 50 per End User. To receive the rebate, you must follow these simple rules and procedures:

1. Fill in (please print) the information on this Rebate Form completely.
2. Mail this Rebate Form along with "proof of purchase" to the address listed below. If you purchase the software electronically, please attach a copy of the "order confirmation" e-mail you received once the software was purchased.
3. This form must be postmarked no later than January 15, 2001.
4. Allow 4 to 6 weeks for processing.

Name: _____

Company Name: _____

Company Address: _____

Telephone Number: _____

Mail Check to: _____

Mailing Address: _____

E-mail Address: _____
Attach copy of "proof of purchase" in the form of receipt and/or invoice.

___ Please do not contact me with other offers and information from Extended Systems.

Mail to: **Extended Systems**
              P.O. Box 6368
              Bozeman, MT 59771
              Attn: Enterprise Harmony Mail-In Rebate

For other information on Extended Systems products, visit our Web site at www.extendedsystems.com.

JetEye *PC* and JetEye *Printer*
Mail-In Manufacturer Rebate

This Extended Systems Manufacturer Rebate is offered to the End User customer who has purchased JetEye *PC* and/or JetEye *Printer* between June 1, 1999 and December 31, 2000. This coupon entitles the End User to receive a check in the amount of $10.00 (U.S.) for each JetEye *PC* or JetEye *Printer* purchased, limit 50 each per End User. To receive the rebate, you must follow these simple rules and procedures:

1. Fill-in (please print) the information on this Rebate Form completely.
2. Mail this Rebate Form along with "proof of purchase" to the address listed below.
3. This form must be postmarked no later than January 15, 2001.
4. Allow 4 to 6 weeks for processing.

Name: _____

Company Name (if applicable): _____

Company Address (if applicable): _____

Telephone Number: _____

Mail Check to: _____

Mailing Address: _____

E-mail Address: _____

Attach copy of "proof of purchase" in the form of receipt and/or invoice.

___ Please do not contact me with other offers and information from Extended Systems.

Mail to: **Extended Systems**
              P.O. Box 6368
              Bozeman, MT 59771
              Attn: JetEye Mail-In Rebate

For other information on Extended Systems products, visit our Web site at www.extendedsystems.com.

www.extendedsystems.com
800-235-7576

Receive 10% off your next TeleAdapt order.*

10% off

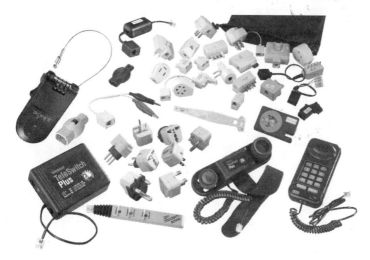

TeleAdapt is the premier supplier of mobile computing products and services for the business traveler. Our comprehensive range of mobile communications devices are designed to get you connected anywhere in the world. TeleAdapt's international telephone and power adapters can get your modem connected in over 250 countries around the world. With our free worldwide 24-hour technical support you can count on us for all your mobile connectivity needs.

Terms and Conditions
*Offer valid on phone orders only, expires December 31,1999.
Not valid in combination with any other promotion. Please reference TELST0399.

O'Toole Business Center
2151 O'Toole Avenue, Suite H
San Jose, CA 95131
Tel: +1 877 835 3232
Fax: +1 408 965 1414
http://www.teleadaptusa.com

Mobile Solutions for the Business Traveler

DEFCON 1

Over 305,000
Notebook Computers
Were Stolen Last Year-
Protect Your Investment
with The Targus DEFCON 1.

$10 Mail-In Rebate
(See Reverse Side For More Information)

The DEFCON 1 Features:
- Versatile, Pocket-Sized Combination Lock
  and Security Cable
- Simple to Use, Difficult For Thieves to Disarm
- Easily Attaches to Your Carrying Case or Any
  Notebook With A Security Lock Slot
- Motion Detector Triggers High-Pitch Alarm
- Flashing LED Lets You Know DEFCON 1 is On
- Audible Chirps Warn of Movement Before
  Alarm Sounds
- 1000 User-Settable Combinations
- 1 Year Limited Warranty

DEFCON 1
$10 Mail-In Rebate

Here's how to get your $10 REBATE:
1. Purchase a Targus DEFCON 1 Security Device from any Targus authorized reseller between May 1st, 1999 and July 30th, 1999.
2. Fill in all the information on this form.
3. Mail completed claim form and supporting sales receipt within four weeks of the sales receipt date to the address on the bottom of this form.

Please Print All Information

Name: _____

Company Name: _____

Address: _____

City: _____ State: _____ Zip: _____

Mail To:

Targus/Sams/$10.00
P.O. Box 100
Placentia, CA 92871-0100

OFFER DETAILS:

Limit one rebate per DEFCON purchased

Offer good only on the DEFCON purchased between May 1st, 1999 and July 30th, 1999

Rebate claims must be made in within four weeks of sales receipt date.

This offer is valid to end user customers only in the 50 United States

Please keep copies of all materials submitted. No responsibility is assumed for lost and/or misdirected mail. No claims against "lost" materials will be honored unless accompanied with proof of receipt.

Targus, Inc. reserves the right to request additional identification/documentation.

Please allow 8 weeks from the last day of the promotion for receipt of the rebate.

Teaches You
Savings In
10 Seconds!◆*

***It only takes 10 seconds to read the coupon below
and learn about a great deal for you!**

Get
20% OFF
The Purchase of
Any PORT Carrying Case or
Notebook Computer Accessory!

Just mention this coupon when you call to order any PORT
Notebook Computer Carrying Case or PORT Notebook Computer
Accessory and You'll Get 20% Off The Purchase Price*. For more
information about PORT products or to order call...

1-800-242-3133

*applicable taxes and shipping charges not included
Offer valid through 6/30/00. PORT is a registered trademark of PORT Inc. © 1999 PORT Inc

Road Warrior Connectivity and Hard Drives Manufacturer Discount

10% off

All connectivity products

Such as the Modem Saver
International Line Tester
and the Telecoupler II
High Speed Acoustic Coupler

Road Warrior Connectivity Products get your laptop
powered up and on line while your on the road. Mention
this ad and receive a 10% discount when ordering any
Road Warrior Connectivity product.

5% off

All Hard Drive Upgrade products

Road Warrior Laptop Hard Drives upgrade your laptop to
capacities up to 14GB with ease. Mention this ad and
receive a 5% discount when ordering any Road Warrior
Laptop Hard Drive Upgrade.

Call (800) 274-4277 or visit www.warrior.com

This Road Warrior International discount is offered to the End-User customer who orders direct from
Road Warrior between June 1, 1999 and December 31, 2000 for one for one of the described products.